THE
BLOUNT REPORT

THE
BLOUNT REPORT

NASCAR's Most Overrated and Underrated
Drivers, Cars, Teams, and Tracks

Terry Blount

TRIUMPH
B O O K S

Library of Congress Cataloging-in-Publication Data

Blount, Terry, 1955–
  The blount report : Nascar's most overrated and underrated drivers, cars, teams, and tracks / Terry Blount.
      p. cm.
  ISBN 978-1-60078-089-9
  1.   NASCAR (Association) 2.   Automobile racing—United States. 3. Automobile racing drivers—United States. 4.   Automobiles, Racing—United States. I. Title.
  GV1033.B56 2008
  796.72—dc22

                                                                2008046799

This book is available in quantity at special discounts for your group or organization. For further information, contact:

Triumph Books
542 South Dearborn Street
Suite 750
Chicago, Illinois 60605
(312) 939-3330
Fax (312) 663-3557

Printed in U.S.A.
ISBN: 978-1-60078-089-9
Design by Patricia Frey
Photos courtesy of AP Images unless otherwise indicated.

For my amazingly loving wife, Tammy, and my incredibly gifted children, Haley and Luke. Writing this book was something all of them encouraged me to do.

Haley was quite the athlete in her high school and college years, reaching surprising heights as a pole vaulter. But she has reached far greater heights as a young woman, making her dad very proud. Haley is now a college track coach, passing along the valuable lessons she has learned in athletics and in life.

My son Luke, a recent college graduate is well on his way to becoming a far better writer than his old man will ever be. What a future he has ahead of him.

This book also for my brother Greg, a huge NASCAR fan and the one person in the world who has traveled the same unusual, and sometimes trying, path in life.

But this book is truly a tribute to my wife, Tammy—my love, my best friend, and my heart. She's the person who listened to all my struggles, all my worries, and lived through all my restless days and nights while researching and writing this book. Never once did she complain. Never once did she become angry. Never once did she walk away and throw up her hands. She patiently stood by me and supported me each day of the process, calmly and lovingly helping every way she could.

This book is dedicated to the people who mean everything to me. It's also a tribute to my mom and dad. They have long since left this Earth, but I hope they know that many of the dreams and aspirations they had for their son came true.

Contents

Foreword

I've been fortunate to work in big-league NASCAR racing for 23 seasons now, broadcasting races on either radio or TV since 1986. And that's just the recent history! I've been a fan of the sport just about my entire life, starting in the late 1960s. In fact, I grew up with a race car in my garage…the cars my dad and his buddies raced at the local short track near my Rhode Island home starting when I was just 6 years old.

My time in NASCAR's big leagues spans a great period. I got in before the greats of my childhood, like Richard Petty, Bobby Allison, and others, retired. I saw Dale Earnhardt, Rusty Wallace, and others of that generation put on some of the greatest races you could imagine. And the newer generation, from Jeff Gordon to Kyle Busch—I've been lucky enough to see them all.

As the sport has exploded in popularity and spread from its beginnings in tiny towns like North Wilkesboro and Rockingham, North Carolina, (both of which I truly enjoyed and miss) to huge, sparkling tracks in mega-cities like Fort Worth and Las Vegas, and even to the hallowed ground of Indianapolis, the one constant has been the thousands of race fans I've met and talked with over the years. They love their sport, they love their drivers…and they're not afraid to speak their minds!

It's been my experience that NASCAR fans are *like* fans of other sports in that they love to talk about and debate the issues, events, and accomplishments of their favorite athletes. But NASCAR fans are *different* from fans of other sports in that their level of passion and commitment to the sport and its drivers rises to a level way beyond any others. Combine that passion with the contents of this book, and there are gonna be some lively conversations, indeed!

In *The Blount Report: NASCAR's Most Overrated and Underrated Drivers, Cars, Teams, and Tracks*, Terry Blount takes on everyone and everything from the sport's all-time great drivers and their accomplishments to tracks, traditions…even the trophies! No one is immune—not The King, not The Brickyard, not even today's most popular drivers. Those things and many more are discussed through the filters of "overrated" and "underrated" with interesting results.

It's not easy subject matter to tackle. It's never easy to call someone overrated…especially, for example, when that someone is the guy who has won the most races EVER! But Terry offers his views and explains his reasoning.

Know this: I don't agree with all of the rankings in this book. In fact, my views differ from Terry's in the very first chapter! But that's the fun of it— batting these ideas back and forth will give you plenty to talk about with your racing friends for quite some time.

Here's a suggestion from me: Before you get started, grab a pen and paper and make your list of the five most overrated and underrated drivers, tracks, races, and records in the sport. Then dive in and see how your lists and reasons match up. Have fun, because that's what racing and this book are all about!

—Allen Bestwick, ESPN

Acknowledgments

From January 2007 through July 2008, I covered 53 racing events for ESPN.com in 20 states and three countries. Trying to write a book while holding down that work schedule proved to be a far more difficult undertaking than I envisioned.

I couldn't have done it without cooperation and patience from some very talented people at ESPN. First and foremost is my boss, ESPN.com motorsports editor K. Lee Davis.

K. Lee is a brilliant journalist. He is also a man with an analytical recall of racing events and drivers that often makes me wonder if someone implanted a reference-book chip in his brain. He's a good old boy from Texas who loves a steak dinner and can spin a fascinating tale with the best of them in between bites of a good rib-eye. His expert opinions and insights were invaluable to me over the course of writing this book, and I'll be forever grateful for his patience and understanding while I labored away.

I also want to thank Patrick Stiegman, ESPN.com's vice president and executive producer, for allowing me to write this book while conducting my duties for ESPN.

I need to give special thanks to NASCAR vice president Jim Hunter, too. No one on the planet knows more about NASCAR and its history than Jim. He has seen it all over the years, and Jim did his best to relate some of those experiences to me.

Jim was an enormous help in listing reasons why he thought certain drivers in the past were underrated. Jim didn't want to say who he thought was overrated—it's not in his nature and not his place as a NASCAR official. I respected that, but he helped me enormously with his thoughts and memories about many drivers.

Introduction

All Racers Deserve Respect

Let's get one thing straight from the start. No one is overrated if they are willing to strap into a race car and risk their life at 200 mph. They have my utmost respect. These are brave people with enormous talent. They have a passion for speed and a desire to control the uncontrollable, taking a dangerous machine and pushing it to the limit.

Driving a race car is a specialized skill that takes years to master. Some are better at it than others. Some are better than people realize. Some aren't quite as good as their reputation. Anyone who has ever sat in the grandstands at a race or watched a NASCAR event on TV has made his or her own judgments.

We all talk about it. Instead of Monday morning quarterbacks, we're Monday morning racers. We strap on those belts, put on that helmet, and know how things should have gone in the race car if we were behind the wheel.

We sit there with our favorite beverage, debating with our buddies and our spouse/significant other (if they will listen) about which drivers ran well and which ones didn't take advantage of their chances to win:

- "That guy isn't as good as everybody thinks."
- "He's terrible. The guy crashes every week."

- "Why doesn't somebody give him a full-time ride? He always runs up front."
- "He's better than the team he's racing for."

This book attempts to make sense of these continuing debates. And it's bound to stir controversy. If your favorite driver is listed as overrated, you obviously won't like it. If your guy is a choice for underrated, you'll say, "Yeah, that's what I've been telling people for years."

Honestly, it's all in fun. There's no intent to ridicule any competitor. This book is not a reflection on how I personally feel about any driver. In fact, some of the drivers listed in the overrated category happen to rank way up there with the best people I've ever met, and some of the underrated guys wouldn't earn points for their friendliness. These lists are based strictly on the racers' on-track performance.

I also need to give a brief definition of both categories. Some people have a mistaken impression on the meaning of the word *overrated*. They equate it with not being good. Not true. In order to fall into the overrated category, a lot of people had to think you were a darn good racer. You can't be overrated if no one ever considered you a top-notch driver. Overrated simply means the overall performance might not have lived up to the general perception of that individual. The reputation doesn't match the statistical compilation, or the hype is more than the data shows.

If overrated doesn't mean a driver was bad, logic tells us the word *underrated* doesn't mean a driver was great. It's an indication that a racer probably was better than some people believe. In this case, the performance was better than the perception. For various reasons, some drivers didn't have the opportunity to prove how good they could have been.

Maybe they only raced part-time, maybe they started too late to make the most of it, or maybe they left us too soon. But one key factor makes rating drivers a far more difficult proposition that rating players in football, baseball, or basketball—it's the car. If you don't have a decent car, you aren't going to win at any level. The best driver will not win in the worst car. The worst driver won't win in the best car. The equipment plays a major part in a driver's success. Consequently, evaluating his skills is a much tougher thing to do.

Making your mark in mediocre equipment is one of the ways a driver moves up in racing. Team owners notice when a guy finishes near the front while racing in a weak car for an under-funded team. They also notice if a driver has a quality ride with a strong team but consistently falls short. Maybe he wrecks a little too often. Maybe it's a pattern of mistakes on restarts. Or maybe he fails to place the car where the equipment logically would place it under normal circumstances.

Some drivers have what baseball officials call "Triple A Greatness." Sometimes a player puts up eye-popping numbers in the minor leagues but can't transfer that success to the big-league level. The same type of thing is true in NASCAR. A driver might be the class of the field in the Truck Series each week, but put him in a Cup car and something changes. His skills don't show up when he's competing against better talent from top to bottom.

Of course, the opposite scenario can also happen. A guy might race a while in the Nationwide Series and look so-so, then he moves to the Cup Series and finds his rhythm with a crew chief and a team that take advantage of his specific skill set.

Jimmie Johnson is a prime example. Johnson came to Cup after an unremarkable showing in the feeder league. But with the help of Jeff Gordon, he got a ride with Hendrick Motorsports and teamed with a brilliant young crew chief in Chad Knaus. Everything clicked.

It also led a few people to question how good Johnson really is. After all, he drives for the best team and has the best equipment. Couldn't you put an average driver in that car and still win? The answer is an emphatic "No." Sure, another driver might win a race or two in the No. 48 Chevrolet, but you don't win back-to-back championships just because you have a fast car.

Evaluating driver skills is a whopping task, even for the most knowledgeable folks in the sport. But I'm giving it a shot, trying to separate fact from fiction, reputation from reality, and equipment from talent.

So, fasten your seat belt and enjoy the ride—it gets pretty bumpy from here.

CHAPTER 1

Drivers All-Time

Some of the 10 names in this chapter may surprise. In fact, if a few of them don't surprise you, check your routine. You're either spending way too much time studying NASCAR statistics, or you really mean it when you say, "Nothing in NASCAR surprises me any more."

The chosen drivers include a few 20-year veterans, an old moonshine runner, a couple of guys who left us all too soon, and probably the most respected man in NASCAR history. All of them played the part and fit into the appropriate category for numerous reasons. Some of them enjoyed remarkable races that rank among the biggest moments in 60 years of NASCAR racing, while others had a long ride at NASCAR's top level without ever making much of an impact.

But when listing overrated and underrated, they all stand out.

Most Overrated Driver
MARK MARTIN

Martin is almost everything a race car driver should be—calculating, cautious, experienced, patient, determined, and remarkably skilled behind the wheel.

But I did say *almost* everything. Martin will probably enter the history books as NASCAR's perennial runner-up. He's the man who always came

Mark Martin climbs into his car at the start of a practice session for the Dover 400 at the Dover Speedway in Dover, Delaware, Saturday, September 23, 2006. (AP Photo/Russell Hamilton Jr.)

close but never quite reached the most cherished prizes of his profession. Many fans believe Martin is simply the ultimate example of bad racing luck.

The two things every NASCAR driver wants most in his career are a Cup championship and a Daytona 500 victory. Martin doesn't have either one, but he still has a chance to earn one or both and prove me wrong.

Martin will go to Hendrick Motorsports in 2009, getting top equipment for a strong chance to win at Daytona—another shot at winning a Cup championship.

But why hasn't it already happened for someone so revered? Maybe it goes a little deeper than just bad luck.

The reason? He's just too nice a guy, a gentleman among barbarians in fire suits. Martin is the anti-Dale Earnhardt. Earnhardt never wanted to lose a race by letting some other driver off the hook; Martin never wants to win a race at another driver's expense.

Martin is known as the guy who always treats his fellow competitors with respect. He won't put someone at risk and force a driver into the wall just to gain one position in a race. He doesn't deliberately tap the rear bumper of the car in front of him to try to win a race, and everyone knows it.

Take, for example, the end of the Nationwide Series race at Las Vegas Motor Speedway on March 1, 2008. Brad Keselowski and Carl Edwards were side-by-side up front, competing for the victory. Martin was behind Edwards on the inside line before the unthinkable happened. Martin ran into the back of Edwards' car, causing Edwards to slide into Keselowski as both cars spun into the wall. Martin went on to win the race.

Had any other driver gone to Victory Lane in that situation, we would have seen one heck of a post-race show. Edwards and Keselowski would have teamed up for a two-on-one ambush on Martin that could have rivaled the infamous 1979 Daytona brawl between the Allison brothers and Cale Yarborough.

But this was Mark Martin. The thought never crossed their minds.

"I'd like to be really mad at Mark," Edwards said. "But he's a heck of a guy and has a lot of respect. I'm sure he just made a mistake."

Martin quickly apologized for causing the incident.

"I ran into the back of Carl, and I hate it," Martin said. "I didn't intend for that to happen."

Drivers say that a lot when they cause a wreck. Usually, no one believes them—but everyone believed Martin. He was driving one of two cars in the race owned by Dale Earnhardt Jr. Keselowski was driving the other one

"We all know Mark's one of the cleanest drivers out there," Earnhardt, Jr. said. "He's taught this entire garage how to drive clean and how to drive respectfully."

Martin has always raced his rivals the right way, and maybe that cost him over the years. He has won 35 races, but the Cup championship has eluded him.

He also has never won the Daytona 500, although some people might argue that point about the 2007 finish. The final lap of that event was a microcosm of Martin's career—so close, but not quite enough.

Martin entered the 2007 Daytona 500 winless in regular-season Cup races on the 2.5-mile super speedway. He had also never won the July event and never won a Daytona 500 qualifying race. His only victory in a Cup car at Daytona came in the 1999 Bud Shootout All-Star event. But it appeared his luck would finally change under the lights on February18, 2007.

Martin was racing side by side with Kevin Harvick as they rounded Turn 4 and headed for the checkered flag. A split-second later, the demolition derby started behind them. A dozen cars were crashing, sliding, tumbling, and burning in their rear-view mirrors.

The two men up front kept the gas pedal on the floorboard, not knowing when the caution flag would fly. Harvick edged Martin by a blink—two one-hundredths of a second, to be exact. It was the closest finish since electronic scoring started and the most dramatic finish at Daytona since the three-wide show at the line 48 years earlier in the first 500. But this one ruined the fairy-tale ending. Harvick reached the line first and left Martin 0-for-23 in the Daytona 500.

"I knew I was going to be the bad guy at the end with Mark leading," Harvick said. "But we kept the pedal down and hoped for the best."

Almost everyone watching the race wanted to see one of NASCAR's favorite sons finally get the dream moment he deserved. Some of them believe it didn't happen because NASCAR broke its own rule. The field is frozen when the caution is thrown. Had that happened at the start of the wreck, many people believe Martin was slightly ahead at that moment and would have been declared the winner.

That depends on when the yellow light actually would have come on. As it turns out, it didn't matter. NASCAR waited until Harvick and Martin crossed the line before throwing the caution.

"I accepted the result about 10 seconds after we crossed the start/finish line," Martin said a week later. "That's how long it took me to get my arms around it. I never gave a thought to the controversy or what could have been. The caution could have come out at a time when I wasn't ahead. Delaying the caution was the right call. It's the last 500 yards on the Daytona 500. Let the leaders decide who wins it." They did, and Martin came up short again. It was a snapshot of his entire career.

Martin was the runner-up to the championship four times over a 13-season span from 1990 to 2002. The one that hurt the most was the first one. Martin lost the title to Earnhardt by only 26 points. But the part that eats at all his fans is the 46-point penalty he received during that season.

NASCAR officials ruled Martin's No. 6 Ford had an illegal part in the engine after his victory at Richmond, Virginia, in the second race of the season. The part was an unapproved carburetor spacer that was half an inch too thick.

Team owner Jack Roush vehemently argued that the part was simply a mistake during the assembly process, and it was clear the spacer provided no performance advantage. NASCAR officials try not to make judgment calls on intent. The part was illegal. That's all that mattered.

No one realized at the time that those docked points would make a difference in which driver won the Cup title. Martin's followers claim he would have won the championship by 20 points had NASCAR not imposed the penalty. Those arguments are flawed because no one can say how things would have unfolded if Martin wasn't penalized. The season had just begun.

It's the same principle as baseball scoring where you can't assume a double play. Would both drivers have raced exactly the same the rest of the way? Would both teams have set up the cars the same? Would both have elected to pit at the exact same moment for each stop in each race down the stretch?

No one can know. Here's what we do know looking at the stats:

- Earnhardt won nine races, including three of the last nine.
- Martin won three, and only one in the last 10.

- Both men had 23 top-10 finishes in 29 races, but Earnhardt had two more top-5 finishes (18 to 16).

Statistically speaking, the deserving man won the title.

Martin's last runner-up year also involved a penalty. He was docked 25 points for an unapproved left front spring after finishing second at Rockingham, North Carolina, two weeks before the season ended.

This time, the penalty wasn't the difference. Tony Stewart won the championship by 38 markers. Stewart had three victories that year; Martin had one. Martin had one more top-10 finish (22 to 21) but Stewart had three more top-5 finishes (15 to 12). Again, the man who ran close to the front more times won the title.

The other two times Martin was the Cup runner-up were complete blow outs, so much so that it's wrong to say he was a serious challenger for the championship. Earnhardt finished 444 points ahead of Martin in 1994 and Jeff Gordon was 364 points ahead of Martin at the end of 1998.

Is Martin the best driver never to win a Cup title? Absolutely, but that doesn't make him one of the best ever, at least not in the top 10. Junior Johnson is the only driver with more career victories (50) than Martin who didn't win a championship, but no one considers Johnson a driver who ranks with the best of the best. Many people see Martin in that light.

Some fans argue that Martin hasn't won a championship because he has never had the best equipment or the best team. They say his five titles in the prestigious International Race of Champions series prove it. Martin out-raced the All-Stars from other leagues in the annual four-race series which pitted drivers in identically prepared sports cars.

What if Martin had raced a Chevrolet all those Cup years instead of a Ford? From 1990 through 2007, Chevy drivers won 12 of 18 Cup champi-onships. Ford won four. However, two of those four titles were won by Martin's teammates at Roush Racing—Matt Kenseth in 2003 and Kurt Busch in 2004. Those were the seasons after Martin's last runner-up finish, so Roush obviously had the cars and personnel to get the job done.

Kenseth and Busch managed to do just a little more to end up on top. In other words, they did whatever it took. But something separated Martin from that logic. Maybe he lacked the killer instinct, or perhaps he just wasn't hungry enough. No one would say that about Tony Stewart or Dale Earnhardt Sr. or even Jimmie Johnson.

The 2007 season was an example of Martin doing things his way. He left Roush's team after 2006 with the intent of racing a partial schedule in the No. 01 Chevrolet for Ginn Racing. But his near-victory at Daytona provided the momentum for his best start in years. Martin posted top-5 finishes in the first three events, and he finished 10th in the fourth race at Atlanta. He was on top of the standings. Many people assumed he would abandon the part-time plan and continue to compete in every event.

At 48 years old, maybe he had another shot at a championship ring. What would Dan Marino, Warren Moon, Karl Malone, or Tony Gwynn give for one last shot at a championship? But Martin had no desire to chase the title again—not at that point, anyway. He stuck to his plan and skipped the next event at Bristol, Tennessee. Sure, it was early. Odds are it wouldn't have worked out, but Martin took a pass at an opportunity, however remote, to change his legacy.

Two years later, he will try it again at age 50. But it wasn't the top of his priority list at the time. Martin opted to spend more time with his family, as he had promised—an honorable decision by an honorable man. It's how he has lived his life. It's how he has raced. Martin never played rough, and that cost him.

One other racer with a similar driving technique fared better. Terry Labonte, who rarely got gorilla with his competitors, won two championships. He led the series in top-5 finishes (17) when he won his first championship for Billy Hagan, out-racing better teams and driving legends such as Earnhardt, Darrell Waltrip, and Bobby Allison.

Labonte's second championship 12 years later came with experience and consistency. Teammate Gordon had 10 victories and Labonte had two, but Labonte won the title by staying out of trouble. He finished 16th or better in all but six events, and only once did he finish worse than 26th.

Labonte found a way to get it done, whatever it took. Martin never quite got the memo. He never found a way to grab the brass ring, partly because he wouldn't reach for it at someone else's expense. It just wasn't his style, and that's not a bad thing.

NASCAR should add an annual sportsmanship trophy and name it after Martin. The Mark Martin Sportsmanship Award to honor the driver who exemplifies class, dignity, and fairness on the track. Who he is as a person, along with his driving accomplishments, guarantees Martin a spot in the new NASCAR Hall of Fame at some point during the next decade.

Fans and drivers respect Martin because of his character on and off the track. But the stats don't live up to how high some people place him in the NASCAR hierarchy. For example, entering the 2008 season, Martin's winning percentage is right at 5 percent. Among drivers with 100 or more career starts, that ranks 44th. It might be surprising to learn a few of the names who rank ahead of Mark on that list—Dale Earnhardt Jr., Cotton Owens, and Ryan Newman.

Among the top 20 in career victories, Martin is one of only three who didn't win a Cup title. Junior Johnson is one and Fireball Roberts is the other. Both men had a winning percentage more than three times higher than Martin. Johnson's winning percentage was 15.92 percent, while Roberts' was 15.38 percent.

Drivers can't be judged simply by races won. Dick Hutcherson ranks 11th in all-time winning percentage (13.59 percent), but no one would consider him the 11th best driver in NASCAR history. Drivers can be judged on whether or not they made the most of every opportunity to win races and championships. On that note, Martin fell a little short.

The Rest of the Top Five
2. GEOFFREY BODINE

It was just Geoff when he won the Daytona 500 in 1986, but Bodine opted for a more formal listing of his first name many years later. Whatever you call him, the eldest of the Bodine brothers was the best of the bunch, but not quite as good as some people believe.

Improving his position on the track wasn't a Bodine trait. In 21 of his 25 seasons, Bodine's finishing spot was worse than his starting position. That's not unusual. Drivers with good equipment who start races near the front often have a finishing average worse than where they started.

That stat really stands out for Bodine. His average finishing position was more than five spots worse than his starting spot in 14 seasons. Three years it was more than 10 spots in the negative. For his career, Bodine's average starting spot was 13.8. His average finishing spot was 18.4. Bodine won 18 races in 570 starts and had 100 top-5 finishes, which is certainly deserving of praise. But he moved backward on the grid too many times.

Here's one key thing in his favor: The man is one hell of a bobsled designer.

3. KEN SCHRADER

This is a much different type of overrated than Martin or Bodine. Those men were winning drivers who many people rank with the best of all time, although that idea seems a little flawed. No one would claim Schrader ranks with the best of all time, but he managed to race full time in Cup for 22 seasons without anyone seeming to care that he rarely ran up front.

Schrader won four times between 1988 and 1991. Yet he raced full time for the next 15 years without winning again. He raced more than eight seasons without posting a top-5 finish. His career winning percentage is 0.55 percent with four wins in 717 starts through the 2007 season.

How does a guy race that long without showing positive results? First, he competed in a lot of bad equipment. Schrader is part of the netherworld of NASCAR—drivers who have long careers but usually run near the back of the pack.

If you're a good guy, show some personality, are good with sponsors, and rarely tear up equipment, you can make a career out of racing at the back. Schrader is the quintessential example. He has raced in all or part of 24 seasons through 2007. If you race a quarter of a century and win in only four of 717 races, you have to be overrated.

4. JEFF GREEN

At least Ken Schrader has won a race. Green can't make that claim. In 265 Cup starts through the 2007 season, Green has yet to go to Victory Lane. Only five times has he finished in the top 5 and only 16 times in the top 10.

Look at it like this: 265 starts are more than seven full seasons of racing. That means Green averaged less than one top 5 per season and about two top-10 finishes per season. Even factoring in some sorry equipment, those are telling numbers. Want a few more? In those 265 starts, Green has led a total of 265 laps, or one lap per start. That doesn't sound so bad, does it?

Well, here's a little comparison using Kurt Busch, a driver with about the same number of starts. In 256 Cup starts through 2007, Busch led 4,633 laps, or 18 times as many as Green.

5. JIMMY SPENCER

This is one heck of a fun guy to be around. He will keep you entertained, because Spencer says whatever he thinks without regard to political correctness. Agree or disagree, he's always interesting. When Toyota was coming to NASCAR, Spencer once said, "You know those guys bombed Pearl Harbor."

On Kelley Earnhardt Elledge, the sister and business partner of Dale Earnhardt Jr., Spencer made this comment on the Speed TV network: "I'm shocked that she kept her middle name. Why keep Earnhardt? I think her ego is so big....and she's not a good negotiator. If she was working for someone else, they probably would fire her."

Yes, Spencer lives up to his nickname, Mr. Excitement. But on the track, it was for all the wrong reasons.

He has one statistic which is similar to Ken Schrader. Like Schrader, Spencer won two Cup races in one season, but never won again. Spencer had two victories in 1994 while driving the McDonald's Ford for Junior Johnson. The rest of his career is all zeros. He raced 12 full-time seasons and parts of five other years without winning. His career winning percentage is 0.42%.

He never ranked in the top 10 in his career. When he won twice in 1994, Spencer ranked 29th in the standings. That's what happens when you fail to finish 11 times in 29 starts, including seven accidents.

That's Mr. Excitement. Other than the two wins, he had only one other top-5 finish and only two other top-10 finishes that season. No one can say

Spencer was afraid to take chances. The man would go for it, sometimes driving beyond the capabilities of his equipment. Spencer failed to finish in 104 of his 478 starts (almost 22 percent) and 54 of those were crashes.

Most Underrated Driver
DAVEY ALLISON

Allison never won a Cup championship. Many people in racing believe he would have won several had he been around to try. We can only imagine how good Allison would have been had he not lost his life in a helicopter crash at Talladega. Looking back at the numbers, Allison's career was zooming upward, and his possibilities for greatness seemed assured.

Davey Allison (left) talks with his father Bobby Allison after a practice round June 18, 1988, at the Miller High Life 500 NASCAR race at Pocono International Raceway in Long Pond, Pennsylvania. (AP Photo/Russ Hamilton)

Allison was 32 when he died in the summer of 1993, right at the age many drivers start their best years as a racer. He had finished third in the standings the previous two seasons, and went into the final race of 1992 with a chance to win the title.

Allison won five races in each of those seasons. He won at Richmond in the third race of 1993 and finished in the top 5 six other times in the first 16 races. He ranked fifth in the standings midway through the season.

He wasn't going to win the championship that year—Dale Earnhardt was running away with it. However, Allison had all the things he needed to win in the future—a team on the rise in Robert Yates Racing (RYR), a respected young crew chief in Larry McReynolds, and most important, he had enormous talent.

It was in the genes for Allison. It was fate. The man was born one day before his father, Bobby, competed in his first Daytona 500 in 1961. Bobby became one of the greatest drivers in NASCAR history and won 84 Cup races. It's not a stretch to say Davey could have been that good, if not better.

Consider this comparison:

- At age 32, after completing his fifth full season in Cup, Bobby had 19 victories and finished in the top 5 in the standings twice.
- When Davey died at 32, he had 19 victories in five full seasons and had finished in the top 5 in the standings twice.

Bobby's sole Cup championship didn't come until he was 45 years old. In the 13 seasons Davey would have had before reaching that age, how many titles could he have won?

This team was on the verge of greatness. Ernie Irvan replaced Davey in the No. 28 Texaco Ford. The year after Davey's death, Irvan was only 27 points behind Earnhardt for the top spot in the standings when he barely avoided death in a horrifying crash at Michigan International Speedway.

Once again, the Yates organization had to regroup from tragic circumstances. After months of rehab, Irvan eventually returned, but he was never the same driver as before the accident.

Six years after Davey died, Dale Jarrett won the championship for RYR. By that time, McReynolds had moved on to Richard Childress Racing as

Earnhardt's crew chief. Had Davey lived, it's logical to assume RYR, Allison, and McReynolds would have teamed up for many successful Cup seasons. The future was bright.

Davey had overcome his biggest weakness—himself. Allison was extremely competitive, but he was also stubborn and headstrong at times. He knew he was good and didn't want to listen to a lot of advice.

In Peter Golenbock's book, *Miracle: Bobby Allison and the Saga of the Alabama Gang*, McReynolds talks about Davey's determination. "Davey was the most determined individual I ever worked with in my life," McReynolds said. "You couldn't get Davey down. The more pressure you put on him, the better he performed."

The 1992 season illustrated that determination when Allison overcame personal loss and serious injuries to almost win the championship. Allison was determined to start the year on a high note at Daytona, a place he knew he could win. In 1988, his first full season as a Cup driver, Allison was the Daytona 500 runner-up to his father in one of the most memorable moments in the event's storied history. Four years later, he won it to start the 1992 season. Everything seemed perfect, but everything changed. His grandfather died that season, and his younger brother Clifford was killed in a racing accident at Michigan in August. Bobby had suffered near fatal head injuries in a crash that ended his career four years earlier.

The '92 season left Davey with injuries of his own to overcome. Davey suffered broken ribs and an injured shoulder in a crash at Bristol a few days before his grandfather died. But the most frightening moment came at Pocono when Allison's car flipped over 11 times after making contact with Darrell Waltrip. Everyone who saw the terrifying accident feared the worst. Thankfully, Allison suffered only a broken arm and wrist, numerous bruises, and a concussion.

That accident allowed Bill Elliott to take over the points lead from Allison, who started the next race at Talladega before allowing Bobby Hillin to take over for him and finish the race in third place.

Three weeks later, Davey experienced the most difficult moment of his life when Clifford was killed in a Busch Series practice session at Michigan.

Davey did what his brother would have wanted him to do and raced at Michigan three days later, finishing fifth. He was only 37 points behind Elliott in the standings.

Allison continued to push. His Ford didn't qualify well down the stretch, but he finished better than where he started in six consecutive races heading to the season's final event at Atlanta. His victory in the next-to-last race at Phoenix gave Allison a 30-point lead over Alan Kulwicki and placed him 40 points over Elliott with one race to go.

Allison was running sixth and in position to win the title with less than 100 laps remaining at Atlanta. Had he finished sixth, he would have won the championship by five points over Kulwicki and 15 over Elliott, who won the race. Kulwicki finished second, but Irvan lost control of his car and spun in front of Allison, who had no chance of avoiding Irvan's car. The championship was lost in an instant.

Allison ended the season with the most top-5 finishes, the most laps led, and he tied Elliott for the most wins at five.

Allison suffered two major injuries that year and got back in the car when most people would have stayed in the hospital. He maintained his focus and won a few days after his grandfather's death, and he kept charging after his brother was killed at Michigan. Does anyone honestly believe a man with that much fortitude, that kind of desire and determination, wouldn't win championships in the future?

Davey Allison would have become one of NASCAR's biggest stars. He would have challenged Earnhardt when the Intimidator won his seventh title. And Allison would have been the man young phenom Jeff Gordon needed to beat when Gordon won three titles in the 1990s.

Earnhardt was once asked in a television interview how good a driver he thought Allison was. "I think Davey would have definitely been a champion several times over," Earnhardt said. "Who knows, I might not have been a seven-time champion if he was still alive. He might have beaten me out a year or two."

The Rest of the Top Five
2. CURTIS TURNER

Even Big Bill France Sr., the man who banned Turner from racing in NASCAR for two years, called Turner "the greatest race car driver I've ever seen." Two-time champion Tim Flock, who raced against Turner throughout the 1950s, said Turner was "the greatest driver ever to race in NASCAR." And Flock didn't say that 50 years ago. He said it in 1997 after seeing Richard Petty and Dale Earnhardt each win seven championships.

Those are some pretty solid endorsements, but for those who need more proof, consider one of the most unusual careers in racing history. Turner was banned from NASCAR for three prime seasons after trying to form a drivers union in 1960. Many of the top drivers were all for it, but France had strong reasons for resisting.

Turner's union backer was Jimmy Hoffa and the Teamsters. Ryan McGee, who wrote a story for ESPN.com, stated that Turner needed financial help after getting $800,000 in debt while helping Bruton Smith build Charlotte Motor Speedway. Hoffa agreed to loan Turner the money if he would help form a drivers' union through the Teamsters. France wasn't a union hater, but he wanted nothing to do with Hoffa. He believed a dangerous gambling element would enter the sport if the drivers formed a union with the Teamsters.

After numerous legal battles, Turner was banned from 1962 through 1964. France finally allowed Turner back in 1965 when Turner turned 41. Turner won once that season, but he wouldn't win again before ending his NASCAR career in 1968.

"In terms of the modern-day world, Curtis definitely is underrated," said NASCAR vice-president and historian Jim Hunter. "He was a superb racer on asphalt, but he was really something to see on dirt. He would throw the car completely sideways in the turns to go in as fast as he could."

Turner is as old-school as they come in NASCAR lore. He learned to drive fast by hauling moonshine on country roads in the Carolinas. Turner was known as a wheelman, the term used for the guys designated to outrun the law with the rot-gut in the trunk.

He transferred those skills to the race track, winning more than 350 races at various levels in his career. Turner never ran a full schedule at the Cup level—known as the Grand National circuit is his day. The one season he came close was 1950 when he competed in 16 of 19 events. Turner won four of those races and finished in the top 5 seven times. His average finish that season was 5.2—good enough to win a title by today's standards—but Turner finished fifth in the standings.

To this day, Turner is the only driver to win back-to-back NASCAR races by starting on the pole and leading every lap (Rochester, New York, and Charlotte, North Carolina, in July 1950). He is also the only driver to win 25 NASCAR races in one season (1956), all in the same car. Twenty-two of those victories came in the former convertible division. Three others came when his team welded a roof on the car, and one of those was the Southern 500 at Darlington.

Why was he so good? The man was absolutely fearless on a racetrack. He was willing to take chances on the track that other drivers wouldn't take. Turner was willing to take chances in life. He's what NASCAR's roots are all about, a former moonshine runner who became an extraordinary racer. He was also a bit of a dreamer, with big ideas that tried to change things. Guys like that are always underrated.

3. DAVID PEARSON

It seems odd to say a man who won 105 Cup races was underrated, but Pearson often doesn't get the credit he deserves for his skills as a racer. But NASCAR competitors know how good he was. In 2000, *Sports Illustrated* asked a panel of 40 prominent NASCAR insiders—a panel that included active and past drivers, team owners, writers, track owners, and TV commentators—who they thought were the greatest NASCAR drivers of the century.

Pearson was a surprising No. 1 on the list, but many fans fail to recall Pearson's greatness. The obvious reason is that his victory total is only a little more than half the number of wins Richard Petty earned in his career.

Take a closer look. Pearson had a higher career winning percentage than Petty (18.07% to 16.86%) and a favorable head-to-head match-up mark.

From 1963 through 1977, Pearson and Petty finished in the top two spots 63 times. Pearson was first in 33 of those races, while Petty finished first 30 times.

The thing that set Pearson apart was his ability to out-think his fellow drivers. Pearson was the most calculating driver of his era, which earned him his nickname—The Silver Fox. Pearson never tried to win a race in the first 50 laps, and he rarely lost one in the last 50.

No one was better at getting the most out of his equipment in the final laps. He always saved his best for last, including the perfectly timed apex pass in the turns. Pearson loved to run high on the track entering a turn, then sharply slingshot downward exiting the turn and zoom by underneath the driver ahead of him.

It was a joy to watch, but we didn't get to see it often enough. Pearson skipped a lot of races when he was at his best. He competed in 75 percent or more of the scheduled events in only four years of his career. But Pearson won the championship three of those years and finished third in the standings the other year.

That's all you need to know.

4. TIM RICHMOND

Richmond competed in only six full seasons before AIDS took his life in 1989 at age 34. In the last 25 Cup races of his career in 1986-87, he won nine times and had 16 top-10 finishes. He finished third in the standings at age 31 in his last full season. His average finish that season was an amazing 4.7. It was his first year with team owner Rick Hendrick and legendary crew chief Harry Hyde, and that was the winning combination Richmond needed to showcase his talent.

No one denies that Richmond could wheel a race car, but few fans today remember how good he was, or how good he could have been. The man was the Rookie of the Year in the Indy 500 in 1980. Richmond is often called the modern-day Curtis Turner because of his all-out style of racing aggressively on every lap. Like Turner, Richmond was one of the few who could race that way and get away with it...most of the time.

Richmond loved the spotlight and wanted his racing career to propel him to Hollywood and acting stardom. It probably would have if Richmond had lived to race when his career was heading toward major success.

5. KURT BUSCH

A lot of NASCAR fans don't like Kurt Busch. The man didn't endear himself to the masses with some of his brash antics at the start of his Cup career. His detractors sometimes mistakenly couple their dislike for him with an impression that he isn't so hot as a driver, either.

Hey, I don't like Barry Bonds, but I have enough sense to admit the man is one of the best hitters of all time, steroids or no steroids. Busch is an amazingly talented race car driver whether you like him or not. Busch finished third in the standings in his second Cup season. He was the series champion in his fourth season.

The 2006 season was a transition period with the move to Penske Racing, but he made the Chase in 2007 and finished seventh. He has finished ahead of Penske teammate Ryan Newman each of his first two years with the Dodge team. By the way, Roger Penske knows a thing or two about race car drivers. If he hires a driver, knowing that driver has a reputation of being brash at times, that driver is probably pretty good.

Busch's early run-ins with Jimmy Spencer, along with his over-aggressive driving and his disputes with NASCAR officials, caused a rift with fans. But he's tried hard to change his image since moving to Penske, although he still comes across as stiff and insincere at times. Busch was accused of drunk driving in Phoenix, accusations that later proved untrue, in a dispute with law officers that led to his dismissal from Roush Racing.

He still has his meltdown moments, like almost punting a Tony Stewart tire changer in a 2007 race when Busch pulled up next to Stewart's car to confront him on pit road. But he usually keeps his composure now. And when he does, he's always a threat to win.

Top 10 Drivers All-Time
1. DALE EARNHARDT

Nothing was more important to Earnhardt than winning races. The seven-time champion would do whatever it took to get to the front. He was three months shy of his 50th birthday when he died, but Earnhardt was still competing for victories and racing up front.

Dale Earnhardt in the garage at the Daytona International Speedway Friday morning, February 9, 2001, in Daytona Beach, Florida. Winston Cup drivers were taking part in their first practice of the 2001 Speed Week. (AP Photo/Chris O'Meara)

2. DAVID PEARSON

His 105 victories gave him a winning average of 18 percent, third on the all-time list of drivers with at least 100 Cup starts.

3. RICHARD PETTY

His 200 victories are misleading by today's standards, but the seven-time champion proved he could race in any era.

4. CALE YARBOROUGH

Winning three consecutive Cup championships in the highly competitive 1970s is reason enough to list Yarborough among the best.

5. JEFF GORDON

Had four championships through the 2007 season, but he would have had two more if NASCAR had stayed with the old points system instead of moving to the Chase format. His 81 career victories at the end of 2007 ranked him sixth on the all-time list, but he's certain to finish at least third by the end of his career and may catch Pearson for second.

6. BOBBY ALLISON

It took him two decades to win the Cup championship, but Allison won plenty of races along the way. The three-time Daytona 500 winner had 84 career wins, 11.7 percent of the races he started.

7. DARRELL WALTRIP

He won three championships over a five-year span in the 1980s, finishing with 84 career victories. Waltrip placed in the top 10 almost half the time with 390 top-10 finishes in 809 starts for 48 percent.

8. TONY STEWART

At the end of the 2007 season, Stewart was still the only driver with championships in both modern points systems the season accumulation system in 2002 and the Chase playoff format in 2005.

9. LEE PETTY

Lee gets overlooked at times because of the accomplishments of his son, but Dad was no slouch. Lee won three championships in the 1950s and tallied 54 victories. In 427 career starts, his average finish was an impressive 7.6.

10. HERB THOMAS

A two-time Cup champion in the early years of NASCAR, Thomas finished with 48 career wins. He has the highest winning percentage (21.1%) among drivers with at least 100 starts.

CHAPTER 2

Daytona 500 Winners

People often compare winning the Daytona 500 to winning the Super Bowl. While it is NASCAR's biggest event, it lacks the championship implications of winning the Super Bowl. There are similarities, but the Daytona 500 is just one race. It doesn't require a series of playoff victories or a winning season to get there. You just show up, try to qualify, and take your chances against 42 other drivers.

A driver can win without being great. It's a little like the guy who caught three passes all season but made 10 receptions in the Super Bowl and scored two touchdowns. Even if he didn't do a single thing worthy of accolades in his entire career, that shining moment in the biggest football game on the planet will forever etch his name into history. The big game has produced MVPs or one-day stars that didn't exactly have Hall of Fame careers—Dexter Jackson, Larry Brown, and Max McGee, for example.

The same thing comes from winning the Daytona 500. You become a member of a very exclusive club. And it's very easy to take that success and overestimate how good a driver really is. Drivers have made long (and financially lucrative) careers off of one or two big moments at Daytona. That's more relevant today than ever before because so much attention is focused on this one event.

It wasn't always that way. Before live national television came to Daytona, a guy could win the 500 and not receive the recognition he deserved. In the restrictor-plate era, Daytona has produced some winners who didn't rank among the elite of NASCAR but have the trophy to show they won the big one.

Professional athletes in other sports roll their eyes when asked, "Would you rather win a most valuable player award or a championship?" The answer is always a championship ring over individual honors. In NASCAR, that question doesn't apply. If you win a Cup championship, you are the most valuable player. It's still a team achievement, but it's also the ultimate individual accomplishment. A championship in NASCAR is not the same as in other pro sports. Baseball players want to win the World Series. NFL players want to win the Super Bowl.

A championship is not NASCAR's Super Bowl because it doesn't have a climactic event. The Daytona 500 is that dream victory, similar to The Masters in golf. Taking the checkered flag at the Daytona 500 is like draining a 3-pointer at the buzzer to win the NBA Finals or launching a walk-off home run to win Game 7 of the World Series—except you don't earn a championship for it. Winning the Daytona 500 is the ultimate single-day achievement in NASCAR, but it doesn't make you a great driver. It makes you a big-time winner on one special day.

Most Overrated Daytona 500 Winner in History
DERRIKE COPE

Maybe we should call Cope the ultimate lucky-win wonder of racing. He's a little like a Super Bowl champion that made the NFL playoffs with a 7-9 record. If Lyle Lovett marrying Julia Roberts is a 10 on the luck scale, Cope winning the 1990 Daytona 500 is a 100. The USA's Olympic hockey victory over Russia in 1980 was less of an upset on the grand scale of sports surprises.

When Dale Earnhardt blew a tire on the final lap, Cope was sitting pretty. Let's give him some credit—after all, the man was running second in NASCAR's biggest race. He would have jumped clear out of his fire suit in celebration had he finished second that February day, but Cope's Lotto

Derrike Cope is introduced at the start of the NASCAR Busch Series Aaron's 312 at Atlanta Motor Speedway in Hampton, Georgia, on Saturday, March 19, 2005. (AP Photo/Glenn Smith)

ticket came in when NASCAR's greatest driver suffered through one of his many heartbreaking moments at Daytona.

Cope was 31, and at a time when his career could have blossomed into something special. He won again that season at Dover, but the rest of his Cup career was all downhill. He never won again after the 1990 season, but one enormous victory goes a long way in NASCAR. Cope managed to milk that accomplishment into a career that included 408 Cup starts. That's a winning percentage of less than one-half of one percent.

Yet Cope is a Daytona 500 champion. Not many men can say that. No one can take it away from him. But the expectations that came from whatever spell was cast to make that magic moment never panned out for Cope.

If not for his Daytona victory, Cope would be one more journeyman driver who passed through NASCAR—nothing special. Nevertheless, his place in sports history is secure for accomplishing one of the biggest upsets of all time. Some list Cope's Daytona triumph right up there among the biggest David vs. Goliath moments ever. Appalachian State defeating Michigan in college football to start the 2007 season, the Miracle Mets of 1969, Buster Douglas knocking out Mike Tyson, and Cope's shocking win in the 1990 Daytona 500. Nice to have a niche among the legendary success stories in sports lore.

You never know where life will take you. Cope dreamed of becoming a big-league baseball player while growing up in Spanaway, Washington, and he had some skills as a high school catcher. He played baseball at Whitman College, suffered a knee injury, and soon focused more on racing.

Cope was in his third full season of Cup racing when the impossible became a reality at Daytona. That day changed his life. Cope raced eight more full seasons in Cup, posting four top-5 finishes during that span. His average finish over those eight years was 23.1.

Cope made more than $9.4 million in his Cup career, mostly thanks to that one day when he made $188,150 for winning the Daytona 500. About $9.1 million of that career total came after his day of glory on the 2.5-mile oval. Even inside traders on Wall Street don't get that lucky. Cope made the most of his big day. More power to him.

The Rest of the Top Five
2. TINY LUND

On a list of heroes and all-around good guys, DeWayne Louis Lund rates as a giant among men, far bigger than his enormous 6'5", 250-lb. body. But on a list of Daytona 500 winners, Tiny comes up a little short.

His victory in the 1963 Daytona 500 is one of the most heart-warming stories in NASCAR history. During a practice session before the race, Lund rescued Marvin Panch from a burning car. Panch, who had won the 500 two years earlier, wasn't able to drive in the race, so he asked Lund to replace him.

Lund agreed, taking over in one of the best cars on the grid, the Ford of Wood Brothers Racing. Lund didn't waste his opportunity and actually won the race. Lund was later awarded the Carnegie Medal of Heroism for saving Panch's life. Lund lost his life 12 years later in a crash at Talladega when he was 45.

From the dramatic Daytona 500 victory until his death, Lund won four more Cup races. He finished with five wins in 303 starts over 20 years. His other four victories all came on short tracks—Hickory, North Carolina; North Wilkesboro, North Carolina; Columbia, South Carolina; and Beltsville, Maryland.

The year he won Daytona Lund finished 10th in the season standings. It was the only time in his career he cracked the top 10. Lund never ran a full season. Only four times in his career did he run at least half of that season's races.

His big day at Daytona came because he saved a man's life. It doesn't get any better than that, but his unselfish act is the reason Lund had the car and the crew capable of winning the big race.

3. MICHAEL WALTRIP

If it wasn't for Dale Earnhardt and his knowledge of building and racing cars on restrictor-plate tracks, Waltrip might still be winless in a Cup regular-season event. Earnhardt gave an old friend the chance of a lifetime when he hired Michael, the Waltrip who isn't Darrell, to drive for him at Dale Earnhardt, Inc. (DEI).

It was an opportunity for Waltrip to legitimize his career—and his career needed some legitimizing at that point. Waltrip was winless in 462 regular-season starts. His only victory came in the 1996 Winston All-Star race at Charlotte. Big money. Cool victory. But not a real event.

Moving to DEI was an opportunity to show he could win on a better team. Waltrip had spent his entire career racing for second-tier (or third-tier) organizations where winning wasn't much of an option. Now he had that option, although DEI hadn't won much either. In its first three seasons as a full-time Cup team, DEI had three victories—two for Dale Jr. and one for Steve Park. Remember, Dale Sr. was driving for Richard Childress, not DEI.

Waltrip became the third DEI driver in 2001. This was his big shot, and he made the most of it. But the biggest day of Waltrip's career was also the darkest day of his life. His first DEI race brought him a victory at NASCAR's biggest event—the Daytona 500. That was also the day Earnhardt Sr. lost his life, blocking on the last lap for two DEI drivers in front of him—Waltrip and Earnhardt Jr.

Waltrip won three more times during the next two seasons, including the 2003 Daytona 500. He won twice in 2002—the spring race at Talladega and the July event at Daytona.

All it proved in the end was that Waltrip could win on the two plate tracks when DEI was dominating restrictor-plate racing. DEI won nine of 10 at the two restrictor-plate tracks from 2001 to 2003. But Waltrip never won anywhere else.

Early in the 2008 season, Waltrip suggested that the much-maligned Auto Club Speedway in Fontana, California, make a radical change of increasing the track's banking to force restrictor-plate racing on the 2-mile oval. It sounded crazy to some folks, but even track president Gillian Zucker thought it might give the place a much-needed identity. For Waltrip, it would mean two more races each year where he could have a chance to win...not that it was a good chance.

Still, four victories in 22 seasons while racing four times a year in plate events doesn't make you the restrictor-plate master. At the end of 2007, after Waltrip's first year as a driver/team owner, he had four victories in 689 Cup starts for a 0.58 winning percentage.

'Nuf said.

4. STERLING MARLIN

Another two-time Daytona 500 winner, but the rest of his career is less than, well, sterling. Marlin had 10 career victories in 732 starts at the end of the 2007 season, a winning percentage of 1.36, or one win for every 73 starts.

It could be worse, as Waltrip proves. But let's take a closer look.

Marlin has raced in Cup for more than 30 years, and he has raced a full schedule for 20 consecutive seasons starting in 1987. He was winless in 15 of those years, but he certainly broke into the win column with the right event.

Marlin's first two victories came back-to-back in the 1994 and 1995 Daytona 500s. When you win the Super Bowl of NASCAR two years in a row, people tend to elevate you to elite status, but Marlin never quite lived up to his Daytona success. Six of his 10 victories came over a three-year span. Five of those were restrictor-plate races at Daytona and Talladega.

Starting in 1997, only once over a 10-year span did Marlin finish in the top 12 in the points standings (he was third in 2001 while driving for Chip Ganassi). The next season was probably the best of his career, but a neck injury in a crash at Kansas ended his year. He led the standings for 25 consecutive races but had faded to fifth before the injury.

Marlin's winning days were over. Marlin didn't win a race from 2003 through 2007 before losing his full-time ride when Ginn Racing sold out to DEI.

5. WARD BURTON

Burton's moment of glory came in 2002 when he found himself in the right place at the right time, working the draft to perfection and leading the final five laps of the 2002 Daytona 500.

Little did he know it would be the next-to-last victory of his career. That wonderful day was the fourth win, which came in Burton's ninth Cup season. He won one last time at New Hampshire that year but didn't revisit Victory Lane after the summer of 2002.

Burton never drove for a strong team, so it's tough to say how good he might have been with quality equipment. But one thing stands out in the negative column—DNFs. Burton had a knack for failing to finish races. He did not finish in 86 of 375 Cup starts through the 2007 season. That's a whopping 23 percent.

In 2007, Burton made 16 starts but posted DNFs in eight of them. Four of those were engine failures, but the other four were accidents. Even in his Daytona 500 winning season of 2002 (his only multi-win year), Burton had nine DNFs, or one out of every four races. As the saying goes, you can't win if you don't finish, and failing to go the distance plagued Burton's career.

Most Underrated Daytona 500 Winner
PETE HAMILTON

One unusual family accomplishment sets Hamilton in a league of his own among NASCAR drivers: His father earned a Ph.D. from Harvard. Pete was no dummy either, figuring out that the best way to win was to drive for a quality team. His 1970 Daytona 500 victory, along with two of his other three career wins, came in cars built by Petty Enterprises.

That Daytona 500 was Hamilton's first race in a second factory car for the Pettys, the stylish blue No. 40 Superbird. No one expected the second Petty machine could compete with King Richard in the No. 43 Plymouth, but Petty blew an engine on the seventh lap in the race. He could have taken over for Hamilton on the next pit stop, but Petty did the honorable thing and let Hamilton stay in the seat—although Hamilton has said many times he wasn't getting out of that race car!

Petty told Hamilton before the race to take it easy and wait until the end to make his move, so Hamilton backed off and took his time most of the day. At the end, he had to outrace another legend. Hamilton passed David Pearson with nine laps to go and won by three car lengths.

Pete Hamilton waves a trophy in victory lane after winning the Daytona 500 on Sunday, February 22, 1970. Hamilton drove a 1970 Plymouth. (AP Photo/CS)

Hamilton followed Pearson into the pits with 14 laps remaining, thinking it was the final stop of the race. Pearson got left-side tires and Hamilton's crew (directed by Petty at that point) changed right-side tires. One lap after they returned to the track, Richard Brooks spun in Turn 2 to bring out another yellow flag.

Petty made a decision to bring Hamilton back on pit road to change the left-side tires, believing four fresh tires could run down Pearson. It wasn't much of a gamble. Pearson and Hamilton were the only drivers on the lead lap, so Hamilton wasn't giving up any track position.

The strategy worked. The last restart came with 10 laps to go. Hamilton quickly got down low and moved inside of Pearson' famous No. 17 Ford. They raced side by side for a lap before Hamilton completed the pass.

It was a major upset, but other drivers soon saw that Hamilton often raced near the front of the field in the second Petty ride. The problem for Hamilton was that the car didn't get the chance to race much.

The Massachusetts native competed part-time for six seasons, winning races in two of them. He drove in only 64 Cup races but posted top-10 finishes is 33 of those outings, including 26 top-5 finishes.

"Desire is the key in racing," Hamilton told the *Inside Florida Racing* radio show in 2007. "It is absolutely crucial to have desire in racing and just hang in there, which I did."

After his Daytona victory, Hamilton became the first driver to win both Talladega races in the same season. But at age 31, Hamilton's Cup career ended because an old neck injury kept flaring up. Another reason for quitting was that he couldn't find a decent ride and had no intention of just making laps.

Hamilton was one of the first Northerners to gain success at NASCAR's highest level. He was called, "The Gentleman Racer" for his polite manner and sophisticated demeanor compared to most people who raced cars for a living.

Hamilton became an accomplished car builder after his racing days ended and later did well as a real-estate investor in Atlanta. But one has to wonder just how good he could have been behind the wheel had he raced 10 more years in good equipment. It wasn't to be, but his victory in the 1970 Daytona 500 was no fluke.

The Rest of the Top Five
2. FRED LORENZEN

Lorenzen was NASCAR's first Golden Boy. Men respected him and women loved him. Dale Earnhardt Jr. has nothing on this guy. His blonde hair and movie-star looks took Lorenzen all the way to Hollywood for a short-lived acting career.

Racing was the thing he did to become a star. He loved the limelight, so he knew Daytona was the place to shine. Lorenzen only raced in the Daytona 500 nine times, but his record in those nine outings is astonishing. Lorenzen finished eighth or better in eight of his nine starts in the big event from 1960 to 1971.

He won the 1965 race and finished second in 1963 and 1967. His average finish was 7.9, but take away his only poor finish—31st in 1964—and his average finish in the Daytona 500 was 3.9. Even after retiring in 1967 at the tender age of 32, he still came back and finished fifth at Daytona in a brief return to racing in 1971.

3. FIREBALL ROBERTS

Roberts' record in the Daytona 500 isn't great. What few people know is that he led more than half the laps he completed in the big race. Roberts only raced in the event six times before losing his life in a 1964 crash. But Roberts, who won the 500 in 1962, ran up front in those early years far more than most people remember.

Roberts still holds the record for most laps led without winning. He dominated the 1961 Daytona 500, leading 170 laps. He had a commanding lead and victory seemed assured before he blew an engine with 13 laps to go, enabling Marvin Panch to go to Victory Lane.

Roberts also started from the pole in 1963 and led 11 laps but blew an engine again late in the race. He started third in 1960 before suffering another engine failure. Mechanical problems kept him from finishing five of his six starts, but he led 365 laps of the 689 laps he raced in the 500 for a whopping 53 percent.

4. BENNY PARSONS

Parsons had his share of bad results in the Daytona 500, finishing 25th or worse in seven of his 20 starts. But he also had some spectacular efforts to go with his 1975 victory. Parsons' win started a string of four consecutive 500s where he finished no worse than third, including a second in 1977. He posted eight top-5 finishes in the event, including runner-up in his next-to-last Daytona 500 in 1987.

His 1975 victory is memorable because he led only four laps. David Pearson had the car to beat but wrecked with less than three laps to go and went spinning down the backstretch. That enabled Parsons to move ahead and win the race.

But Parsons never would have gotten there without help from Richard Petty. The King was having a bad day, at several laps down, but he hooked up with Parsons in the draft to enable Parsons to reduce Pearson's big lead. Parsons slowly began reeling in Pearson through lapped traffic. If Petty couldn't win it, he wanted Parsons to beat Pearson.

Not sure what that shows more clearly: How much Petty liked Parsons, or how much he didn't like Pearson? You'd be hard-pressed to find anyone who didn't like Parsons. He had a long and successful broadcasting career after his racing days ended, passing away in 2007 after a battle with cancer.

5. BUDDY BAKER

Baker was at his best at NASCAR's two fastest tracks—Daytona and Talladega—in the days before restrictor plates were added to slow down the cars. The man should have been a fighter-jet pilot. The faster they ran, the better he raced. His skills were magnified when most drivers backed off because things got too dicey at more than 200 mph.

Baker posted 12 top-10 finishes, including eight top-5 finishes, in the Daytona 500, and he won it in 1980. To this day, it's the only Daytona 500 completed in less than three hours with a record average speed of 177.602 mph.

His first Daytona 500 was 1961, and his last was 1992 when he finished 11th at age 51. Baker's early years at Daytona weren't successful. He didn't earn a top-10 finish until 1969, but he had nine top-10 finishes over a 12-race span from 1977 through 1988. Baker also won the 1983 Firecracker 400 at Daytona.

The only thing faster than Baker on fast tracks was his ad-lib skill in the broadcast booth, as he quickly came up with endless one-liners that made him a fan favorite. One of his best came moments after watching a Truck Series racer crash in a turn: "He ran out of talent about halfway through the corner."

Baker never ran out of talent during the super fast days at Daytona.

Top 10 Daytona 500 Winners All-Time
1. RICHARD PETTY
Earned a remarkable seven victories over a 17-year span. He's the only man with more than four Daytona 500 wins and one of only two drivers with more than three. Petty also led the race in 20 of his starts.

2. CALE YARBOROUGH
At his best on the biggest stage, Yarborough was a four-time winner in the 500 over a 16-year span.

3. JEFF GORDON
Compiled three Daytona 500 victories through 2007, and in 1997 at age 25, he was the 500's youngest winner.

4. DALE JARRETT
Who can forget the dramatic call by father Ned Jarrett in the broadcast booth when he saw Dale head for the finish line to win his first Daytona 500 in 1993? Jarrett went on to win the event two more times (1996 and 2000).

5. DALE EARNHARDT
He only won it once and it took him 20 years, but Earnhardt's victory ranks as one of the most dramatic moments in NASCAR history. Earnhardt was

Richard Petty cheers with his free hand as he holds the Governor's Cup after winning the NASCAR Daytona 500 at the Daytona International Speedway in Florida, on Sunday, February 14, 1971. (AP Photo)

the master at winning other Daytona races, too. He won 34 times on the 2.5-mile oval, including 12 qualifying races, seven Nationwide events, six Bud Shootouts, six IROC events, and two Pepsi 400s.

6. LEE PETTY

You can't leave out the man who won the first Daytona 500 in 1959. But Petty didn't know he was the winner until three days after crossing the line in a three-way photo finish for the inaugural event.

7. BOBBY ALLISON

Won the big show three times, including a dramatic victory over son Davey in 1988. Allison was also involved in one of Daytona's most memorable moments, the infield brawl he and brother Donnie had with Cale Yarborough after a last-lap crash in 1979.

8. BILL ELLIOTT

Won it twice over a three year span (1985-87). Elliott is one of only eight drivers to win the Daytona 500 more than once. He also turned the fastest official lap ever recorded at Daytona—210.364 mph in 1987, the year before NASCAR went to restrictor plates.

9. MARIO ANDRETTI

He was the first Indy car driver to win the world's biggest stock car race. Andretti's 1967 Daytona win came two years before his only victory in the Indy 500 and 11 years before his Formula One championship.

10. A.J. FOYT

He already had three Indy 500 victories (1961, 1964, and 1967) when he took the checkered flag in the 1972 Daytona 500. He also won the 24 Hours of Daytona and is the only man to win both Daytona events, the Indy 500, and the 24 Hours of Le Mans.

CHAPTER 3

Speedways

So what is it you really want when you go to a NASCAR race? Do you want a comfortable seat where you can see most of the track? Do you want a speedway location that gives you access to nice restaurants and entertainment options at a major market?

Do you want a campground that makes it easy to set up your stuff and shoot the bull with fellow campers? Or maybe a place where the party gets a little rowdy, like Talladega? Do you want a place where traffic problems are minimal (sorry, no such thing for Cup races) or at least a major highway to get in and out of the facility?

Maybe all you need is great racing, even if everything else about the place resembles some dusty West Texas bleachers for a six-man high school football game. That's not enough for some fans, who want a taste of the good life—luxury suites, gourmet food, private clubs, exclusive up-front parking, etc. Choosing speedways for overrated, underrated, and top notch overall requires factoring in a little bit of all those elements.

Sprint Cup races are held at 22 speedways across the country, from rural Virginia to suburban Los Angeles. Each track has its highs and lows. Some facilities don't receive enough credit, while others get far too much.

NASCAR's List

Back in 2003, NASCAR commissioned a private research firm for a two-year study to determine which speedways were the most beneficial to the sanctioning body. The study—done by an unnamed New York firm—considered fan avidity, market size, seating capacity, television ratings, and exposure for sponsors.

The study ranked 32 tracks overall, but included here are the results for the tracks that host Cup events:

- Indianapolis Motor Speedway
- Lowe's Motor Speedway
- Daytona International Speedway
- California Speedway
- Texas Motor Speedway
- Chicagoland Speedway
- Bristol Motor Speedway
- Las Vegas Motor Speedway
- Michigan International Speedway
- Talladega Superspeedway
- Kansas Speedway
- Dover International Speedway
- Phoenix International Raceway
- Atlanta Motor Speedway
- Homestead-Miami Speedway
- New Hampshire Motor Speedway
- Infineon Raceway
- Pocono Raceway
- Watkins Glen International
- Richmond International Raceway
- Darlington Raceway
- Martinsville Speedway

Well, they got one thing right. Martinsville deserves the bottom spot. Other than that, I beg to differ. Pocono and Watkins Glen ahead of Richmond? What were they rating—track length? And two of those top five have serious issues, as explained later in this chapter. So take a seat, grab a beverage, and see how your favorite tracks rate.

Most Overrated Speedway
AUTO CLUB SPEEDWAY

It was formerly known as California Speedway, but this place needed more than a name change. Few things infuriated old-school NASCAR fans more than moving the Southern 500 from Darlington, South Carolina, to California, giving the two-mile Fontana oval the Labor Day weekend event in 2004.

The field of the NASCAR Auto Club 500 passes the main grandstand at the two-mile oval of California Speedway in Fontana, California, on Sunday, May 2, 2004. (AP Photo/Chris Carlson)

NASCAR officials had logical reasons for the relocation. They wanted two Cup races a year, including the holiday weekend, in the country's second largest market. Because Darlington wasn't selling out both its races, even though the Lady in Black has only 60,000 seats, it seemed to make sense at the time. So did the Edsel and leisure suits.

Adding a second annual Cup race for the Fontana facility hasn't worked. Even in a market of 15 million people, ACS can't fill all 90,000 seats for the Cup races.

NASCAR didn't do the track any favors when it scheduled February and early September dates for those events. NASCAR managed to give ACS two dates where the temperatures were either above 110 degrees or below 60. It may be a warm breezy day in Malibu, but Labor Day weekend at Fontana can rival the Sahara desert. The 2007 weekend saw temperatures that reached 115 degrees. Now doesn't that make you want to drive out there and sit in the stands for four hours?

The February race weekend in 2008 had constant rain, windy conditions, and temperatures in the low 50s. Hey, isn't this supposed to be the perfect weather of Southern California? Yes and no. Fontana is part of the Inland Empire, home of the middle-class masses of "Cali." L.A. it ain't—and that's the problem.

Officials for NASCAR and International Speedway Corporation (the track's parent company) envisioned this facility being the track of the stars, a way for NASCAR to gain new fans with Hollywood celebrities. NASCAR desperately wants to court the Hollywood crowd to show up at the races, but having the Auto Club 500 on the same day as the Academy Awards isn't the way to do it.

NASCAR makes the schedule, not the speedways. Surely in this case, any other weekend is preferable to Oscar weekend when the movers and shakers in Tinseltown have other things on their mind. Scheduling a stock car race in Southern California on the same day as the biggest event of the year in L.A. leaves something to be desired in marketing strategy. The Tinseltown media aren't rushing out to Fontana when they have their own version of the Super Bowl taking place on the same weekend.

NASCAR communication director Kerry Tharp said in 2007 that NASCAR sees it as an opportunity to take advantage of a big weekend in Southern California.

"A lot of people are in L.A. this weekend that wouldn't normally be here because of the Academy Awards," Tharp said. "It's a chance to get some of those people interested in the NASCAR races."

That's like asking kids to take an interest in a popsicle on Christmas morning.

The race isn't a direct conflict time-wise, but casual fans aren't going to make the trip east to Fontana—about a 50-mile trip on I-10 from downtown L.A.—to watch a race and risk missing part of the Oscars telecast. And don't forget the pre-Oscar hype on the tube—preview shows on the red carpet and the annual *Barbara Walters TV Special* with her questions for the big stars.

You might say that people who care about racing don't care about the Academy Awards. For some hardcore fans, maybe that's true, but NASCAR isn't in California to appeal to the hardcore fans. There aren't enough of them. NASCAR wants the stars involved.

A few celebrities always make an appearance. Kevin Costner gave the command to start engines at a 2007 race. Comedian Brad Garrett did it a year later, making fun of Kyle Busch's ears in the process. But most of the beautiful people in Beverly Hills spend that Sunday getting ready for their biggest day of the year. Race cars don't enter their thought processes. The only car they care about is the stretch limo that will drop them off at the red carpet.

There's no red carpet to roll out among the abandoned warehouses of Fontana. The speedway doesn't have the amenities to attract up-scale casual fans. Luxury suites (a stretch to call them luxurious) are few.

Trying to sell ACS as being in the shadow of Tinseltown requires an acting job worthy of an Academy Award. The celebs gracing the covers of gossip magazines have never been to Fontana, unless passing through on a drive to Las Vegas. This facility is 55 miles east of Hollywood, 60 miles from hip and trendy Santa Monica, and 75 miles from Malibu.

Fontana has about as much in common with Beverly Hills as Talladega does with Monte Carlo. Jet set celebrities aren't lining up to buy tickets for a race at ACS. It's doesn't help that the on-track competition hasn't been top of the line, either. So the pure NASCAR fans, those who only want to sit in the stands and watch good racing action, don't even have that as an enticement.

ACS president Gillian Zucker deserves enormous credit for working 24–7 to make the Fontana facility what everyone envisioned it could be. She has connections in Hollywood, keeps a positive attitude, and tries dozens of promotions to remake the image of the speedway. Zucker opened an office last year in Century City near the major movie studios to gain more attention from the Hollywood elite. At the time, Zucker said she wanted the California Cup races to become "the toughest ticket in town" — a lot to ask in a city overflowing with entertainment options.

Nothing has panned out to turn things around, but a few adjustments could improve things. First, change the dates to increase the opportunity for good weather. Instead of Labor Day weekend, a race inside the Chase would stir up attention.

That idea becomes a reality in 2009 when ACS finally moves off Labor Day weekend for a Chase race in early October. ACS worked out a three-way swap, sending Atlanta Motor Speedway the Labor Day weekend event. Talladega takes Atlanta's late October Cup race, and ACS takes Talladega's early October event.

But the February event at ACS remains one week before the Cup race at Las Vegas Motor Speedway. Having those races back-to-back almost begs people to choose one or the other. If you live in L.A. and have the means, flying to Vegas one week later is a preferable plan to driving more than an hour in traffic to watch a race at Fontana.

Improvements to the racing surface should also help. The track had the dreaded "weepers" during the rain-postponement in February 2008, with water seeping up through the turns. Michael Waltrip suggested ACS add banking and make the two-mile oval a restrictor-plate track to set it apart from the other speedways out West. Even Zucker liked that idea, but ISC officials aren't going there.

As bad as things have gone, team sponsors still want two races at ACS. They get more for their money in a big market. For example, Lowe's has more than 50 stores in the Los Angeles market. It has only 42 stores in the entire state of South Carolina. Television networks also want races in bigger markets. Sports events in major markets get higher TV ratings than smaller markets because more people in that market watch an event in their area.

If the Fontana races continue to have problems selling out, some traditional NASCAR fans will continue to say, "I told you so." But they are missing the point. Selling all the seats isn't the big concern for sponsors spending million of dollars in Cup.

They want exposure in the big markets. Races near L.A., Chicago, Dallas-Fort Worth, Kansas City, and Phoenix deliver that exposure far better than Darlington, Martinsville, or Pocono. It would help tremendously if NASCAR could pick up the entire facility and move it closer to L.A. If Dodger Stadium was in Fontana instead of Chavez Ravine (in the shadow of downtown L.A.), attendance would suffer.

NASCAR officials want races in the L.A. area to draw more Hispanic fans to the sport. Officials would also like the early California date to capitalize on the buzz generated by the Daytona 500 the previous week. The Daytona winner always travels to New York to make the rounds on the TV shows before flying to L.A. to garner media attention in the country's second-largest market the week of the Fontana race.

There are far worse facilities than Auto Club Speedway. Access in and out of the track is as good as any speedway in NASCAR. It has ample parking, an enormous infield, and grandstand seats that offer a view better than most tracks this large. But as far as living up to its billing, the Fontana track isn't close to reaching the checkered flag.

The Rest of the Top Five
2. INDIANAPOLIS MOTOR SPEEDWAY

The late Bill France Jr. made one of the best decisions of his career when he agreed to race stock cars on the storied Indy grounds. Taking NASCAR to

The Brickyard in 1994 brought 250,000 spectators, the biggest crowd in the history of the sport. It proved fans would accept cars with fenders making laps on the giant rectangle.

It was the right thing to do, but no event gets more attention with less action than the Cup race at Indianapolis. Big stock cars and the narrow flat pavement at Indianapolis don't mix well. The combination makes for some pretty boring races around the four corners of the old speedway.

The success at Indy did a tremendous favor for NASCAR. It proved NASCAR was a viable sport on a national scale. NASCAR's fortuitous move to Indy came only a couple of years before open-wheel racing in America nearly destroyed itself.

The split between CART and the Indy Racing League, which started in 1996, severely damaged the prestige and popularity of the Indy 500 at a time when NASCAR was on the rise. Open-wheel's 12-year war played into the hands of NASCAR when the sport was becoming mainstream, partially from the success at Indy. But the people who actually watched the Cup event at Indy soon realized it was short on drama and long on single-file racing.

IMS is the largest sports facility in the country. It's also one of the oldest. The track has 257,000 seats, as painstakingly counted by *Indianapolis Star* reporter Curt Cavin a few years ago. But many of those quarter-million seats offer some downright crappy viewing. The sightline of the track is limited, fans can't see the backstretch from the frontstretch, and you can't see much in the turns if you're sitting near the famous row of bricks at the start-finish line.

A lot of people don't care. Seeing everything on the track doesn't matter. They go because it's Indy. It's the racing Mecca. All racing fans should go there at least once. But if you make the trip, do yourself a favor—go to the Indy 500, not the Allstate 400.

3. POCONO RACEWAY

This archaic track in the hills of Pennsylvania has two Cup races a year for one reason only: It's a mere 85 miles from New York City.

Until someone finds a financially viable way to build a speedway in the country's No. 1 market, or someone buys Pocono and moves races elsewhere, this fossil of a race track will continue to play host to two races that are too long, too boring, and too far behind the times for where speedway amenities are today.

At least NASCAR could do the racing world a favor and shorten these Cup events from 500 miles to 400. The triangle-shaped track in Long Pond is 2.5 miles around. Making 250 laps (750 turns) on this course takes an eternity. It also doesn't help that for years NASCAR has scheduled the two Pocono events less than two months apart. Must we repeat this torture twice in the same summer?

"It's outdated and needs a ton of upgrades," Jeff Gordon said in 2008. "The fact that it's in the Northeast is a positive, but I'm shocked it has had two [Sprint Cup] races as long as it has. I'd be surprised if it stayed that way for the future, just because of other markets where we need to be."

Pocono is a little like going through a time machine to a speedway of the past, mainly because the place hasn't changed much in 40 years. Some might call that vintage. This isn't wine, folks. The place is the trifecta for speedway hell: backwoods location, bad facility, and boring racing.

4. MARTINSVILLE SPEEDWAY

Martinsville is NASCAR's oldest track. It shows.

Short-track racing has its place and often produces exciting competition, but this track is no Bristol. Martinsville is a flat half-mile oval with tight turns. If you're on the outside, you're slowing down. But you do see plenty of bumping and banging, which many fans love about short-track racing. That's why Martinsville has it place on the Cup schedule, but it doesn't need a race twice each season.

This is as backwoods as it gets, a prime example of NASCAR's rural Southern roots. It's hard to get to, and once you're there, it's hard to find a decent place to stay. It's also smaller than advertised. For years, Martinsville officials listed the facility with 90,000 grandstand seats. When the track was sold to International Speedway Corp. as part of the legal settlement with Texas Motor Speedway, the actual seat total was announced at 60,000—33 percent smaller than its reputation.

Martinsville's long history in NASCAR is the reason it should keep a race. But the track would have lost one of its two annual Cup events already had ISC been successful in its efforts to build new tracks in New York and Seattle. It's only a matter of time before those new tracks are built with better facilities and better racing than Martinsville can provide.

5. WATKINS GLEN INTERNATIONAL

The Glen is America's most historic road course, but 57 years of history shows in this facility. Watkins Glen has its charms from days past, but it no longer ranks among the better road course facilities in the country.

NASCAR has a better option just north of the border in Montreal. The famed Circuit Gilles Villeneuve played host to a Nationwide (still Busch then) event for the first time in 2007. The island course drew a huge crowd and produced exciting racing and a controversial finish when Robby Gordon was black-flagged after punting the leader, then pretended he won the race with doughnuts at the finish line.

It was a heck of a show in a major international market, something NASCAR officials have said repeatedly is part of their plan. But The Glen remains part of the schedule for political reasons. It's an ISC track, and ISC is controlled by NASCAR's France family. They aren't going to take a race away from themselves.

The solution? ISC should try to buy the Montreal course, or some other more suitable road course, and leave Watkins Glen for the history books.

Most Underrated Speedway
TEXAS MOTOR SPEEDWAY

One year and one week after Texas Motor Speedway opened, TMS president Eddie Gossage was ready to give up. Gossage had lived through two infamous NASCAR weekends where almost everything that could go wrong did go wrong, so he offered his resignation to Speedway Motorsports Inc. chairman Bruton Smith.

Racers follow the pace car before the start of the Samsung/RadioShack NASCAR 500 race at the Texas Motor Speedway in Fort Worth, Texas, Sunday, on April 17, 2005. (AP Photo/Donna McWilliam)

"I knew he needed a scapegoat," Gossage said. "So many bad things had happened and so much bad publicity had come from it. Maybe Bruton would be better off with someone else in charge. Maybe it would turn things around. I told him I would resign and things would get better, but he wouldn't even consider it."

Smith didn't become a billionaire by making bad leadership decisions. He knew he had the right man in charge. "I told Eddie I had total confidence in him," Smith said in 2006. "He can have a 50-year contract as far as I'm concerned. I told him something I learned a long time ago: To belittle is to be little. People kept taking shots at us, but a lot of it was jealousy."

Smith knew what people were saying, calling TMS "Bruton's Folly." They were calling Gossage many other unflattering things.

In the *Dallas Morning News* story of 2006, Gossage remembered that former NASCAR chairman Bill France Jr. didn't have any kind things to say about him during the second NASCAR weekend in April 1998 when the racing surface was leaking water. "Mr. France said he would fire me if I worked for him," Gossage said. "That was the absolute low point."

Things have made a dramatic turnaround since those dark days. TMS is the only example in this book of someone or something going from most overrated to most underrated in a matter of a few years. This 1.5-mile oval 20 miles north of Fort Worth has emerged as one of the top success stories in all of motor sports.

No speedway opening in 30 years was hyped and anticipated more than the debut weekend of TMS in 1997. It was promoted as the Taj Mahal of racetracks, the best of the best. No expense was spared. This was Smith's showplace, a facility that would change the stereotypical image of many NASCAR speedways as rickety grandstands way off the beaten path.

All the glittering talk became rampant criticism on the opening weekend. Smith's North Texas palace was a muddy mess after torrential downpours throughout the area during the week of the event. Most of the parking lots hadn't been paved in time for the first race, so grass lots became unusable quagmires. A few folks in the media center were referring to the facility as "Gossage Bay."

More than 200,000 patrons showed up on Sunday for the Cup race, curious what this NASCAR stuff was all about. For some reason, it seemed to catch TMS workers and Fort Worth law enforcement officials by surprise. Only one traffic pattern existed—a dead stop.

The water-logged grass lots left no place to put many of those cars. People parked where they could, which included Interstate 35. Cars lined both shoulders of the highway. Fans gave up on driving into the facility because they sat for hours without moving 100 yards. And if you did make it into the TMS lots, you regretted it when the race ended. Getting off the grounds took hours as workers had no idea how to direct traffic, which was moving in every direction but out.

It was miserable to sit in a car, off the track and on it. The guys in the race cars were complaining the loudest. The original layout at TMS was a complete failure. The race started with a 13-car pileup in the first turn of the first lap. When they did get around to Turn 4, drivers found the exit off the turn too sharp, causing several crashes into the outside wall.

"I've tried to forget all that," Gossage said. "I should have done hours of therapy. That first year was ugly and embarrassing." And the second year wasn't any better. The rains came again and caused water to seep through the track in Turn 1. After a couple of crashes, qualifying was canceled.

Bill France Jr. threatened to cancel the event, but cooler heads prevailed. The driver complaints were endless, many using a new word to describe the track: "Unraceable." That led someone to print up T-shirts that read, "Shut-up and Drive." Fans could buy them at the track. Almost everyone accused Gossage of instigating the T-shirt plan, but he swears he had nothing to do with it. The drivers were lining up against him, but one driver gave Gossage the benefit of the doubt.

When Mark Martin won the second Cup race at TMS, he motioned for Gossage to walk over to the car before Martin got out. Martin asked Gossage if he was serious about fixing the track. Gossage gave Martin his word on it.

"OK, then I'm going to take the heat for you," Martin told Gossage.

Martin stood in Victory Lane and said on national TV that the track was okay and people needed to stop worrying about it. "I can't tell you how much that meant to me," Gossage said. "Mark was the only one who came to my defense. I will never be able to thank him enough." Martin was inducted into the Texas Motorsports Hall of Fame in April 2008.

Smith spent more than $4 million in 1998 to completely reconfigure the racing surface, and said he would do whatever it took to make TMS the best racing facility in the country. Part of the Turn 4 wall was moved back to make the exit out of the turn an easier transition. A new drainage system was installed under the track to prevent "weepers" from coming up through the asphalt in wet conditions.

"We dusted ourselves off and stayed in the game," Gossage told the *Dallas Morning News.* "It was a lot like being a pro expansion team. You go through some bad years, but you stick with it and stay the course."

It worked. The racing improved each year:

- Elliott Sadler edged Kasey Kahne by half a car length at the finish of the 2004 TMS race.
- Jeff Burton made a last-lap pass to become the first two-time winner in the spring race of 2007.
- Jimmie Johnson and Matt Kenseth raced a side-by-side, paint rubbing battle for the lead in the final laps of the fall race in 2007 before Johnson won it.

The track that no one could race on is now a track where everyone wants to race.

TMS finally received its second annual Cup date in 2005 after a long and bitter lawsuit with NASCAR to acquire it. Texas still produces some of the biggest crowds in Cup—more than 150,000 attend each Cup event, and more than 100,000 attend the Nationwide races.

Few tracks offer as many amenities to the fans as TMS. Its campgrounds are the best in the country, but TMS also caters to the well-to-do with hundreds of luxury suites above the frontstretch; a $30 million, nine-story Speedway Club with a ballroom overlooking Turn 1; and an 11-story condominium tower in Turn 2.

"There's nothing that can come close to what we have here," Gossage said.

That may be a bit of stretch with the recent improvements made at Las Vegas Motor Speedway, but TMS has nothing to feel embarrassed about now. Some people still remember those early years and how bad things were, so they underestimate how much things have changed.

It was a hard road to get there, but Texas Motor Speedway has become the spectacular facility that Smith and Gossage always wanted it to be.

The Rest of the Top Five
2. LAS VEGAS MOTOR SPEEDWAY

Things were going pretty well at Las Vegas Motor Speedway when track owner Bruton Smith decided to spend some money in 2006 to make it better. The track was reconfigured from limited banking to a high-banked oval, similar to Texas and Atlanta, two other 1.5-mile tracks in the Speedway Motorsports Inc. empire. But Smith added a special twist on this redesign—The Neon Garage. It's a modernistic design for crews and fans, this diamond-shaped Cup garage with a fan zone in the middle. Fans can walk upstairs and look down on the crews at work.

The setting for the track is breathtaking with mountains on each side of the facility. But it's not the mountains that bring the masses to this place. It's that beaming Strip about 12 miles south of the track—Vegas, baby. America's playground. Plush hotels, extravagant casinos, glitzy shows, and a race. Now that's a vacation. More people come to this race from other parts of the country than any other event on the Cup schedule.

LVMS is a modern facility with everything a fan could want, including a man-made plateau outside the backstretch where patrons can park RVs and watch the race.

The racing hasn't proved spectacular yet, but it's likely to improve as the new surface ages. This is one heck of an entertaining place, on and off the track.

3. PHOENIX INTERNATIONAL RACEWAY

How many places can you sit on the side of a hill, have a picnic, and see everything that happens on and around a 1-mile racetrack? That little oddity is one of many unusual assets that Phoenix International Raceway has to offer. It has a short-track feel in a big-market atmosphere.

PIR is different from any other track in NASCAR. It's one mile around, but not a true oval. The backstretch has a bend in it, almost like a dogleg. Turns 1 and 2 are a little tight, but Turns 3 and 4 are long and sweeping. The track is relatively flat, which makes it tricky to drive but loads of fun to watch.

And when you're through watching, one of the most dynamic cities in the West is waiting to entertain you. If you can't find anything interesting to do in Scottsdale, you just aren't trying. The track is only 20 miles west of downtown Phoenix. Traffic is a big issue at any Cup event, but PIR has much easier access to and from the facility than most NASCAR venues. NASCAR deservingly gave PIR a second annual Cup date in 2005, but few people back East realize it's one of the best stops on the schedule.

PIR is an older facility. Some renovations were done a few years ago, but more changes are needed to bring it up to par with the latest amenities. Even without those changes, this track is still a great place to watch a race.

4. HOMESTEAD-MIAMI SPEEDWAY

It took three tries to get it right, but the 1.5-mile oval in South Florida now has one of the most competitive racing surfaces of all the intermediate ovals in NASCAR. Since its opening in 1995, Homestead-Miami Speedway has undergone two reconfigurations of the racing surface. It started as a flat rectangle but was converted to more of an oval shape two years later.

That didn't change much. The racing was still awful. So HMS officials changed it again to add additional banking in 2003, but it wasn't just more banking. The track went with a new concept called progressive banking. The track is gradually banked more steeply toward the outside wall. This concept has helped produce more side-by-side racing.

More banking means faster speeds, but the higher groove is the longer way around. You go faster, but you have a little more ground to cover than a driver on the inside line. That makes for good racing, and the Homestead track has shown it in recent years. It's been a good setting for the final race of the Chase, even though the facility has only 75,000 seats.

This is one of the few places NASCAR can race in mid-November and have a good chance for comfortable weather conditions. The Homestead facility is out in the boonies among palm-tree farms, but it's only a short haul up the toll road to Miami Beach and all it has to offer.

5. INFINEON RACEWAY

A road course underrated? Such a thought is sacrilege among some NASCAR traditionalists, but the 12-turn course in the heart of the

California wine country deserves some love. It's a magnificent setting, and believe it or not, the racing is pretty interesting. This place has a uniqueness that real racing fans enjoy, even if some oval-only supporters can't see it.

Road racing is a specialized skill that requires timing, daring, good judgment, anticipation, and car control. A driver can't win on the 1.99-mile Sonoma layout without possessing all those characteristics.

It's rare to get to the end of a race at Infineon where the dreaded hairpin turn doesn't come into play and decide the leader board. That's the toughest part of the course as drivers head to the start-finish line, but it's also the place to make a pass if a driver gets inside the car ahead of him.

This venue is bigger than one day of racing. It's only 35 miles north of downtown San Francisco, one of the great cities in North America. Or fans can stay in the Sonoma area and tour the various vineyards, sampling some of the best wines in the world. The facility has only 47,000 seats, but who needs a seat when you can sit on a hillside and hear the roar of 43 stock cars racing by?

Some people involved in NASCAR would like to see the road courses eliminated from the Cup schedule. Don't do it. Cup drivers should test their skills in a different discipline. It's the right thing, and while we're at it, NASCAR should move this race inside the Chase. The Cup champion should have to race on a road course during the 10-race playoff.

Top Five Speedways
1. DAYTONA INTERNATIONAL SPEEDWAY

No place screams NASCAR more than Daytona. Its opening in 1959 signaled a new era in stock car racing, a time when high-speed super speedways became the sport's calling card. Daytona is the only facility in any sport where the biggest event of the year—the Daytona 500—starts the season.

What's Good

1) The biggest race in America, the Daytona 500, now far exceeds the Indianapolis 500 in popularity.

NASCAR drivers take the green flag to start the Daytona 500 race on Sunday afternoon February 18, 2007, at the Daytona International Speedway in Daytona Beach, Florida.
(AP Photo/Chris O'Meara)

2) The breathtaking drama of restrictor-plate racing, where the cars are bunched together in large packs and the unexpected can happen at any moment. Fans love it; drivers hate it.

3) Major renovations in 2005 made the infield an amusement-park atmosphere, including new garages with large windows so fans can look inside and watch the teams work.

4) The beach and the Atlantic Ocean are only 10 minutes away.

5) A major airport is a stone's throw away. The main runway is directly behind the backstretch.

6) Walt Disney World is a one-hour drive away.

What's Not

1) International Blvd., the main road in front of the facility, is busy when there isn't a race taking place. It becomes total gridlock before and after races.

2) Many improvements and expansions have been made over the years, but the facility is 50 years old and shows its age in some places. Some fan comfort and amenities are not up to speed compared to newer tracks.

daytona facts

Location: Daytona Beach, Florida
Track size and shape: 2.5-mile high-banked tri-oval
Metro area population ranking: 102
Closest Top 50 market: Orlando (29), 50 miles west
Spectator capacity: 185,000

2. BRISTOL MOTOR SPEEDWAY

Bristol is the Rose Bowl of racing. Drivers have described racing at Bristol as flying a jet fighter in a gymnasium. More than 160,000 spectators fill the tiny track, which is unique in all of motor sports. It was a virtual demolition derby of 500 laps with constant bumping and banging before the track was resurfaced, which brought better racing but fewer wrecks.

What's Good

1) A close-action show in the most unique setting in racing. The facility is deafening once the race starts. The grandstands form an enormous bowl that holds in the noise and the exhaust fumes. The decibel level, the smell and the fact that cars make a lap in 15 seconds can have a dizzying effect on the spectators.

2) A great view from almost every seat. You feel like you are looking down on a giant slot-car track.

3) The most avid fans in NASCAR. All 160,000 seats are sold in advance for every Cup event.

What's Not

1) Not the easiest place to get to in the northeast corner of Tennessee.
2) Limited hotel space is ridiculously overpriced.
3) Almost takes an act of Congress to get a ticket to a Cup event.

bristol facts

Location: Bristol, Tennessee

Track size and shape: .533-mile high-banked concrete oval

Metro area population ranking: 178 for Tri-Cities of Bristol, Kingsport, and Johnson City

Closest Top 50 market: Charlotte (37), 120 miles southeast

Spectator capacity: 160,000

3. RICHMOND INTERNATIONAL RACEWAY

Richmond is the only three-quarter-mile track in Cup. It's a wide surface with a D-shape and limited banking that produces some of the best racing in NASCAR. And you don't have to leave town to see it. Heck, you don't even have to leave the neighborhood.

What's Good

1) Short-track racing on a Saturday night at its best. A wide track with limited banking produces loads of passing and bumping.
2) Plays host to the race that decides the 10 drivers who make the Chase for the Nextel Cup.
3) Not a bad seat in the house and it's easy to follow the action all the way around the track.

What's Not

1) The inner-city location has no major highway access, which can cause traffic delays.

2) An old facility that opened in 1946, but it has undergone many expansions and renovations.

---

richmond facts

Location: Richmond, Virginia
Track size and shape: .75-mile flat oval
Metro area population ranking: 46
Spectator capacity: 110,000

---

4. TALLADEGA SUPERSPEEDWAY

Some fans affectionately call Talladega the "Redneck Riviera," a place where the hard-working man can see which drivers have the guts to get it done. NASCAR's biggest, baddest, and most dangerous track has to rank among the best. Talladega is one of a kind, sort of a Daytona on steroids, and it's a place where you have to man-up, on and off the track.

What's Good
1) Dramatic pack racing where cars are inches apart at 190 mph on the giant oval that tests a driver's courage and drafting skills to get to the front.
2) A huge campground that becomes a community within itself. And the community activities are guaranteed to get a little rowdy.
3) Good access from Interstate 20 allows fans to make the trek east from Birmingham or west from Atlanta.

What's Not
1) This is no place for the wine-and-cheese crowd. Dega is NASCAR at its blue-collar best and not a place to make business deals in a luxury suite.
2) Things have gotten out of hand at times, with angry fans throwing beer cans on the track after the hated Jeff Gordon won, so you need to watch your back.

talladega facts

Location: Talladega, Alabama
Track size and shape: 2.6-mile tri-oval
Metro area population ranking: Not ranked in the top 200
Nearest Top 50 market: Birmingham (48)
Spectator capacity: 160,000

5. LOWE'S MOTOR SPEEDWAY

This track is a prime example of how an old facility can renew itself and keep up with the times. The concept of upscale accommodations started here with the visionary minds of track mogul Bruton Smith and world-class promoter Humpy Wheeler.

What's Good
1) The heart of NASCAR country, where many of the biggest names in the sport got their start.
2) The facility is 49 years old, but you wouldn't know it to look at it. It has all the bells and whistles of the newest speedways in the country.
3) Side-by-side racing with lots of passing.
4) NASCAR's biggest test of endurance, 400 laps in the Coca-Cola 600.

What's Not
1) The original of the many so-called "cookie-cutter" tracks, the 1.5-mile ovals.
2) The track's biggest event comes on the same day as the Indy 500.

lowe's facts

Location: Concord, North Carolina (20 miles north of downtown Charlotte)
Track size and shape: 1.5-mile quad-oval
Metro area population ranking: 37
Spectator capacity: 180,000

CHAPTER 4

Play by the Rules

NASCAR rules are in a constant state of fluctuation. Stick around a while, and you'll see them change. That's not necessarily a bad thing. NASCAR officials make adjustments based on how the sport evolves. They also try to stay one step ahead of the competitors.

The goals of all teams in the garage include finding ways to circumvent the rulebook and gain some type mechanical or aerodynamic advantage. Some would call that cheating. Crew chiefs say they're only stretching the envelope and looking for loopholes. Whatever. The point is this game of cat-and-mouse gets progressively more difficult to enforce as technology becomes a bigger part of NASCAR.

It's not for a lack of trying—cheating is just a whole lot harder to do. The window of opportunity is shrinking as the cars become almost identical through engine, body, and chassis regulations.

The so-called Car of Tomorrow, which was introduced in 2007 and became the only car in Cup one year later, was designed to eliminate most of the gray areas. Some crew chiefs, especially the ones who often found ways to outsmart the inspectors, say NASCAR has gone too far and stifled creativity.

The bodies of the four manufacturers are almost identical except for the decals. The areas where teams can make approved adjustments have been significantly reduced. But you didn't really think this would stop guys from cheating did you? Excuse me, I mean finding an edge.

After Carl Edwards won his second consecutive race early in 2008, a post-race inspection showed that the lid of the oil-tank reservoir inside the car was off. That seemingly insignificant problem could have given Edwards an aerodynamic advantage. NASCAR imposed the dreaded double-100 penalty—100 points taken from Edwards and a $100,000 fine for crew chief Bob Osborne, along with a six-week suspension. Of course, team owner Jack Roush claimed it was an innocent mistake, nothing more than a part failure. That goes with the territory.

No one has *ever* cheated in the glorious history of auto racing. They may have done plenty of other things: Pushed the envelope, worked in the gray areas, outsmarted the other guy, tweaked the car and invented new applications. And sometimes, just for fun, they stuck it to the man.

But cheated? Never. Doesn't happen, not in the eyes of the racers.

Bending the rules is easier in auto racing than other sports for one simple reason—the car. The main instrument of the sport is a complex piece of machinery with thousands of parts in various sizes and shapes, each with a specific task. Sometimes all it takes is a small alteration of one part to achieve the desired effect of improved performance. Maybe that's cheating. Then again, maybe it's innovation. However you see it, NASCAR has more of it than all the other racing leagues combined.

And NASCAR officials hate it. NASCAR wants to eliminate the perception of hayseeds breaking rules just for fun. It's a false perception. These guys aren't hayseeds. They are some of the best engineers in the world using millions of dollars worth of advanced technology.

These brilliant guys have state-of-the-art computers, wind tunnels, and highly specialized mechanical devices to find any possible edge when hundredths of a second can make the difference between winning and losing. Sometimes you find something a little outside the lines of conformity. The racers say it's just part of the process. NASCAR says it's breaking the rules.

The 2007 season started at Daytona when five teams received penalties. But the big one went to Michael Waltrip's new Toyota team. Inspectors found some type of fuel additive (officials never revealed the substance) in the car's manifold. The crew chief and the team vice president were sent home, banished from the Daytona 500. The same thing happened to Chad Knaus, Jimmie Johnson's crew chief, in 2006, but Johnson still won the Daytona 500.

Breaking rules is far less prevalent today than it was a generation ago when the saying was, "If you ain't cheatin', you ain't tryin'."

There was the infamous Darrell Waltrip scam when his crew chief, Gary Nelson, rigged the car with a device to release buckshot on the parade lap, reducing the weight of the car as Waltrip told his crew, "Bombs away, boys." Waltrip and A.J. Foyt used nitrous oxide to boost horsepower in qualifying for the 1976 Daytona 500. And don't forget the legendary moment when NASCAR inspectors removed the gas tank from Smokey Yunick's car before watching him drive off without it.

That type of blatant cheating is absurd by today's standards. Breaking the rules now is done in tiny increments. A team might modify the body of the car by a fraction of an inch to try to gain 20 pounds of downforce. Or they might alter the fuel tank just enough to gain one more lap on the track without pitting.

Most of the time, it doesn't seem worth the risk. But the teams keep trying, and NASCAR keeps increasing the punishments. Catching violators is only one aspect of NASCAR's long list of rules and regulations. Some of the sport's most controversial rules have nothing to do with cheating.

Believe it or not, every NASCAR rules decision was made with a goal of fairness. Sometimes it doesn't work out that way, and changes are required. Those changes don't always come soon enough.

Here are few that stand out:

Most Overrated NASCAR Rule
GUARANTEED SPOTS IN THE FIELD

Make a lap, and take your chances. That's how it should be in qualifying, but Cup racing is divided between the haves and the have-nots. Most of the drivers who show up each weekend know they have a guaranteed spot in the field regardless of what happens in qualifying—the ones who don't have to try to earn a spot in a system that's stacked against them.

Qualifying has become NASCAR's unwanted stepchild. The top-35 rule, the one that guarantees a starting spot to the top 35 teams in owner's points, is a complete failure for many reasons.

The rule has created a weekly procedure that is unfair to some and almost meaningless to others. There is no incentive for top 35 cars to emphasize qualifying. Where a racer starts has little correlation to where he finishes at many tracks. If 50 cars show up for a race, 15 of those drivers are vying for only eight spots—seven if someone gets in on a past champion's provisional. It means a driver can post a faster speed in qualifying than other drivers who make the race on a guaranteed spot and still not earn the start.

That's just downright un-American.

The rule was put in place to protect teams that show up every week, along with their sponsors. It didn't work that way in 2007 when Toyota brought new teams to the series with big-money sponsors. Most of them were showing up every week and going home, failing to earn one of the few spots available to them in qualifying.

That doesn't even account for the problem of a Friday rain-out. If weather conditions caused NASCAR to cancel the qualifying session, no attempt was made to reschedule it the next day. Some drivers who didn't have a guaranteed spot in the race were forced to pack up without ever making a qualifying run.

Why not let the drivers without a guaranteed spot, the go-or-go-homers, make a qualifying lap and compete for the last eight spots on the starting grid? At least that way they have a fighting chance.

This illustrates just how little qualifying means to NASCAR. It's become a rote process that needs a major renovation. NASCAR and the teams value practice sessions over qualifying, opting not to reschedule qualifying on Saturday morning if it means eliminating a practice. But it's qualifying that has a Victory Lane celebration and bonus check for the pole winner. Maybe that should go to the fastest driver in practice.

Practice sessions are extremely important to the race teams, giving them needed feedback on the car in race conditions. But they should not be held at the expense of fairness to the drivers hoping to make the field. If practice is mandatory, set the field based on practice session speeds. That's usually a far better indication of how a team will do in the race than qualifying.

NASCAR took a baby step in the right direction at the start of the 2008 season when the non-qualified cars were grouped together in a qualifying session. The group placement made it easier for the fans to understand who was fighting to get in. It also helped to ensure the non-qualified drivers were making their qualifying attempts under similar weather conditions. But it isn't enough to correct the problem.

If it rains on Friday, the non-qualified drivers are out of luck, even though NASCAR usually still has another day before the race to try to give these racers a qualifying attempt.

The 2008 Auto Club 500 at Fontana, California, was a situation where the drivers never got a chance to make the field. Qualifying was rained out Friday, so the 43-car field was set based on a complicated points allocation format utilizing results from the 2007 season. It's inexcusable that NASCAR set the field without giving the 13 go-or-go-homers a chance to get in by making qualifying laps on the 2-mile Auto Club Speedway oval the next day. It meant five drivers—Ken Schrader, A.J. Allmendinger, Patrick Carpentier, Burney Lamar, and Mike Skinner—packed up and left California without any opportunity to make the race.

Saturday's schedule was tight because the Nationwide Series and the Craftsman Truck Series were racing a rare NASCAR version of a double-header. The schedule was also revised because of Friday's wet conditions. But NASCAR never reschedules qualifying for the next day. It would take less than an hour for 13 non-qualified drivers to make two laps and attempt to qualify. The go-or-go-homers could vie for the final eight spots. In this case, one of those spots automatically went to Kurt Busch as a past Cup champion, so he could have skipped it. That drops it down to only 12 cars vying for the final seven spots.

All of them would gladly accept that option over a system that fails to give them a chance to earn it with a qualifying lap. Giving drivers a chance to make the race on the track should always take priority over setting the field on points.

The Rest of the Top Five
2. POINTS FOR LEADING A LAP

This is the cheapest five points in all of racing. The rule might make sense if NASCAR changed it to say a driver earned points for taking the lead under green flag conditions, but handing out five points for leading a lap is nonsense, a reward for doing nothing.

A driver can run at the back of the field but get five points for staying on the track while all the cars in front of him come to pit road under a caution flag? It's recognition of non-achievement. No one deserves a bonus for leading a lap under caution.

This situation is worse now with the Chase format. A driver who isn't in the 10-race playoff can allow a teammate who is in the Chase to pass him for the lead and get the five bonus points. So a driver could win the Cup championship because a teammate gave him a free pass to the front.

NASCAR also awards five bonus points to the driver who leads the most laps, which is fine. You can't fake your way to those points. But an extra five markers for leading one lap is often a phony ploy to get the lead when a driver has no shot to run up front under actual racing conditions.

3. NOT ENOUGH POINTS FOR WINNING

The NASCAR points system is all about consistency. It sounds good, but it really means you don't have to win to stay near the top of the standings. As long as a driver finishes in the top 15 every week and avoids a bad finish, he's going to stay near the top of the standings—and it's possible to win a Cup championship without winning a race.

NASCAR has taken small steps to rectify the problem. A few years ago, the formula was so preposterous that the second-place finisher actually could earn as many points as the winner if the runner-up led the most laps. That flaw was changed by giving the winner 10 additional points, but it's still an insignificant amount for beating 42 other drivers.

NASCAR took another step in the right direction in 2007 when it seeded the Chase drivers by victories in the regular season. Each victory was worth 10 points. Consequently, winning mattered more in the first 26 races. The flaw was that the 10 playoff races reverted back to the regular points system. Again, winning wasn't as important as earning top-5 finishes and making sure you avoided a DNF along the way.

The problem hasn't burned NASCAR yet. Jimmie Johnson won four of the last five races in the 2007 Chase, even taking a few chances to win when he didn't need to risk it. But it was great to see him go for the win instead of being content to finish fifth and collect the points.

However, that doesn't change the fact that the formula still fails to place enough emphasis on winning.

4. DAYTONA 500 QUALIFYING

Neither NASA scientists nor MIT mathematicians could explain all the ramifications of this ridiculously convoluted system. Even if they could, you'd fall asleep before they finished the lecture. Some drivers don't get it. I call it the Rubik's Cube of NASCAR qualifying.

It starts with Pole Day the week before the race. Single-car qualifying for any restrictor-plate race is three hours of your life you'll never get back, but this one has even less significance since only two spots are determined. The front row is set on Pole Day. Actually, two other drivers earn a spot based on their Pole Day speeds, but that's way too complicated to explain without a slide rule.

Besides those lucky guys, everyone else learns their starting spots based on the Duel races four days later. A good idea in theory, but it doesn't work that way in reality. First, the Pole Day snoozer. As Tony Stewart has often said, "A monkey could do it." It takes one full lap to get up to speed with the restricted engines, then one lap with the pedal to the floor in hopes that your guys found a little more horsepower than everyone else.

After 55 cars or more make a couple of incredibly boring laps around the gigantic 2.5-mile oval, two drivers celebrate being on the front row. The rest move to the Thursday afternoon qualifying races.

Important things are happening in two races, but it's almost impossible to know for sure what they are while the cars circle the track. Figuring out who gets in and who doesn't from the Duel races makes your head spin faster than a loose car in Turn 2.

The concept of racing your way into the field is a good one, but at least 35 drivers start the Duel races knowing they have a guaranteed spot. Only a handful of drivers in each qualifier are trying to earn one of the eight available spots on the starting grid (seven if someone has a past champion's provisional he can use).

Strategy for the qualifying races depends on where a driver falls in the Cup food chain. The game plan for the non-qualified drivers is desperation: "Gotta get to the front." For some of the drivers with a guaranteed spot, it's about preparation: "Let's see how this car works in the draft." But for most drivers, it's salvation: "Don't wreck my ride, people!" Drivers who know they have a strong car and just want to avoid the carnage that's lurking around every turn when others are frantically pushing the limits to earn a spot in the 500.

It takes a program, a rulebook, a stat list, and a little knowledge of each participant to figure out who falls into each category. For the fans, it's total confusion. When each of the 60-lap races end, the fans are left wondering who got in. The top two finishers in each Duel among the non-qualified drivers earn spots. But if the two drivers that made it in on lap speeds from Pole Day are in the top two in their Duel race, it opens up a spot for someone else. Confused yet?

If NASCAR really wants some drama, it should put all the non-qualified cars in the same Duel event. Now that would be a sprint race worth watching. Putting all the guaranteed drivers in one Duel and all the go-or-go-homers in the other would certainly increase the drama and allow the fans to know immediately who earned a spot in the field. Finish in the top eight, or go to the house.

An even better idea would be to eliminate the top-35 rule and make every driver earn a spot. Unless I miss my guess, neither option is coming anytime soon. Apparently simplifying this system makes too much sense.

There is some good news. Every driver has a chance to race his way into NASCAR's biggest event, which is more than they can say anywhere else.

5. IMPOUND RACES

NASCAR officials came up with a plan a few years ago to try to save money for the Cup crews. The cars would be impounded after qualifying, so that the teams couldn't make any major adjustments after qualifying ended.

The idea was to save money. It doesn't. The only way to save money for the teams is to cut the number of days at an event from three days to two, eliminating a day of hotel charges and meals for the crews.

Impound races penalize the cars that don't have a guaranteed spot in the field. The teams that have that luxury qualify the car in the race set-up. They are willing to give up a little speed in qualifying to make sure the car is ready to go when the race starts the next day.

But the teams without a guaranteed spot have to set up the car in qualifying trim to get every bit of speed from the car on one flying lap. The problem is they have to start the race with the qualifying set-up because the cars are impounded immediately. Adjustments are needed on the first pit stop to get the car into race trim.

Impound races at Talladega have also caused the odd situation of the slower cars starting up front—not the safest way to begin a race where the cars run in large packs only inches apart. The quagmire of impound-race qualifying on a restrictor plate track was clear for everyone at Talladega in the fall race of 2007. For example:

- A.J. Allmendinger and Boris Said, the ninth and 10th fastest drivers on speed, respectively, did not make the 43-car field.
- Dale Jarrett, the No. 8 qualifier, started last when the green flag flew Sunday. That's a rule. The slowest qualifier who didn't have a guaranteed spot has to start in the back.
- The top eight qualifiers, including pole-winner Michael Waltrip, were drivers who ranked below the top 35 in the season standings.
- Five drivers in the top 15 in qualifying speed didn't make the race. Three drivers in the Chase—Jeff Gordon, Kyle Busch, and Kevin Harvick—ranked in the bottom nine on qualifying speed.

Welcome to the backward world of impound qualifying at Talladega. This is how it works out if you have teams on completely different agendas when qualifying begins. Qualifying for a top-35 team in this situation means absolutely nothing, because those teams have a guaranteed spot in the field. At an impound race, they work on the race set-up and blow off qualifying adjustments. But the teams that don't have a guaranteed spot have to concentrate on making the car as fast as possible for qualifying. They set up the car to run at maximum speed for two laps alone on the track.

It isn't the best way to go fast in a big pack of cars once the race starts, so the top 35 teams blow off trying to gain speed for qualifying. It's an embarrassment to the sport and a cheapening of the show for the people who pay money to come to the track and watch qualifying when most of the teams don't have to take it seriously.

It's also unfair to the drivers trying to make the field with a strong qualifying effort. Waltrip won the pole in the October Talladega race, a far better result than he had in the spring event. Waltrip was 20th in speed out of the 52 drivers who made a qualifying attempt, but he didn't make the race. Twenty-four drivers who posted a slower qualifying lap than Waltrip made the field. Waltrip's speed was 190.045 mph in the No. 55 Toyota. Here's how crazy it gets—Paul Menard was the driver one spot ahead of Waltrip in speed at .034 seconds faster, but Menard made the race and started 19th.

Jeff Burton's qualifying lap was only 186.579 mph, but he wasn't really trying. He had a guaranteed spot. Why waste time on qualifying trim when you're going to change 20 spots in 10 laps anyway in a restrictor-plate race?

Most Underrated NASCAR Rule
THE CHASE PLAYOFF SYSTEM

This is the rule all the old-school NASCAR fans love to hate. But it beats the heck out of the alternative, which was a boring stretch where no driver has a realistic chance of catching the points leader.

Consider the 2007 season as a prime example for all you Chase haters. Jeff Gordon had a 317-point lead in the Cup standings. Any realistic chance of catching him wouldn't exist without the playoff format. Gordon could have coasted home, continued to post top-10 finishes, and easily won his fifth championship without anyone seriously challenging him.

As we all know, it didn't turn out that way. Jimmie Johnson won his second consecutive title. It was fun to watch as Johnson won four consecutive races in the Chase to stay in front of his teammate. We saw a much more exciting battle for the championship than we would have seen without the Chase.

Under the old format of a single points total for the entire season, Johnson's win streak wouldn't have been enough. Johnson won the title by outracing Gordon at the end. That's how most sports championships are decided.

Obviously, there was a huge downside to the Chase format for Gordon. It cost him the championship for the second time. But it's better to have 12 drivers with a chance to win the crown in the final 10 races than one driver who can coast home to the title.

The Chase format has other benefits as well, including one that could have helped Gordon in the regular season. He made a decision to be with his wife, Ingrid, and miss a race if she went into labor on a race weekend. Mark Martin was ready to fill in for Gordon in the No. 24 Chevrolet if Gordon was busy at the hospital.

It turned out that wasn't necessary because Gordon's daughter was born on a Wednesday, but missing a race is a new option for championship contenders at certain times in the season. If a driver is securely in the top 12, he can skip an event if needed for an important family matter. It's another positive side of the Chase format.

He could also sit out a race from an injury and still be a contender for the title. If a driver has a severe ankle sprain from an accident in an event and is solidly inside the top 12, he could choose to stay on pit road for the next race.

In the past, drivers with injuries often started a race when they had no business wheeling a race car. That driver would run a couple of laps, or wait until the first caution, then get out and let a replacement driver take over.

Whoever started the race earned the points for that event, so drivers felt compelled to get in the car and tough it out for a few laps. Now, even if he isn't in the top 12, a driver still has the option of skipping a race if necessary and hoping to make up the points to get back to the top 12 before the Chase begins.

He couldn't make up 500 points to get to first, but he might make up 50 points to get back to 12th. Obviously, this doesn't help the 12 contenders once the Chase begins, but at least the option is available before the playoff starts.

Detractors say the Chase doesn't produce a true champion that accumulated the most points for an entire season. Following that logic, the New York Giants weren't the true champions of the NFL by winning the 2008 Super Bowl. The title should have gone to the New England Patriots because they went undefeated in the regular season.

Even college football, as bad as the Bowl Championship Series mess is as a phony playoff, at least tries to match up No. 1 against No. 2 in a one-game playoff.

In an age where there's so much competition for the entertainment dollar, and at a time when the attention span of many fans is measured in seconds, not weeks, days, or even hours, having some type of playoff is essential to keep most fans interested.

The Chase doesn't provide a guarantee that the final race will have several drivers in contention for the championship. A driver can still build a big points lead in the final 10 races. There are also no guarantees the World Series will go seven games and be decided in the ninth inning. It might be a four-game sweep. But at least the winner had to legitimize their championship by beating the best of the best at the end.

The same thing is true in the Chase. You have to prove you deserve it by outracing the other contenders down the stretch. That didn't always happen in the old format.

The Rest of the Top Five
2. THE S.A.F.E.R. BARRIER AND HEAD-AND-NECK RESTRAINTS

The S.A.F.E.R. barrier and head restraints are 1A and 1B in the NASCAR Renaissance of Safety since Dale Earnhardt's death in 2001. It takes both of

Gary Nelson, NASCAR's managing director of research and development, left, talks with Humpy Wheeler, president of Lowe's Motor Speedway in Concord, North Carolina, as they examine a portion of the S.A.F.E.R. barrier being installed at the track Wednesday, April 21, 2004. The barriers, which are made of rolled steel tubing and use foam blocks, will cover 6,100 feet of the concrete walls around the 1.5-mile speedway. (AP Photo/Chuck Burton)

them working together to revolutionize the sport and make fatal injuries a thing of the past.

It seems ludicrous now to think that slamming head-on into a concrete wall was an acceptable safety device in racing for decades. After Dale Earnhardt's death, people finally started to consider the possibility of using collapsible barriers around the outside boundary of race tracks.

But many of the leading authorities in NASCAR believed it couldn't be done. The theory was any so-called "soft wall" would do more harm than good. In a glancing hit, which is often the case on an oval track, a cushioned barrier would snag the car and hold it, causing other cars to run into it.

Even if that problem could be overcome, how would NASCAR officials be able to repair the damage to the cushioned wall in a reasonable amount of time during a race?

Dr. Dean Sicking, a scientist at the University of Nebraska and the leading authority on roadside safety, had answers for both of those problems. Sicking and his team developed the Steel and Foam Energy Reduction (S.A.F.E.R.) Barrier. It is unquestionably the single greatest advancement to safety in the history of auto racing. I list it here as underrated because some people in the sport don't understand how remarkable an achievement it is.

The barrier is a relatively simple design that is built in front of the concrete walls. The S.A.F.E.R. barrier is stacked hollow steel tubing in front of foam padding. When a car hits the barrier, it bends, greatly reducing the G-forces of a high-speed impact. It also rarely needs repairs after an impact, but when it does, the sections are easily replaced.

The S.A.F.E.R. barrier wasn't universally accepted at first. Some people in NASCAR felt the additional depth of the barrier (about 18 inches) would cause more accidents because it made the tracks narrower and would take away the racing groove up high. Some track promoters balked at the expense of adding the barrier (about $3 million on a 1.5-mile oval), but how do you put a price on a driver's life?

All speedways that play host to NASCAR events now have the S.A.F.E.R. barrier in the turns, but NASCAR officials need to take it a step further and require placement of the barrier on all exposed concrete walls at a track.

It's impossible to say for sure how many lives have been saved due to the barrier during the last five years, but drivers have often made head-on impact with the collapsible wall and walked away without a scratch. Some of those collisions had a greater G-force at impact than the accident that killed Earnhardt.

The Head-and-Neck Support (HANS) Device and the variations of that system are a vital part of the safety advancements. The restraints connect the driver's helmet to the back of the seat, stopping the neck from snapping forward violently at impact. NASCAR requires all drivers to wear some form of the head restraint.

Earnhardt's death was caused by a severe basilar skull fracture when his head snapped forward. This was a common cause of death in many racing accidents involving head-on collisions. Head and neck restraints keep the head in place at impact.

3. GREEN-WHITE-CHECKERED FINISH

For 55 years, NASCAR fans had to take their chances, and hope the yellow flag didn't fly near the end of a Cup race. If it did, you could hear the moans in the grandstands, and some guy watching at home probably threw his beer can at the TV.

The late yellow meant the event would end without a race to the finish. The cars would crawl across the finish line behind the pace car, bringing a huge buzz kill for everyone who invested the previous three hours in watching the show.

In the summer of 2004, NASCAR officials finally realized there was a better way. If a caution came out before the final lap, the competitors would get one shot at a two-lap finish under green. It has become one of the most popular rule changes NASCAR has ever made. Fans want to see a race end with, well, racing. Even if it means added laps to the scheduled distance, so be it.

Since the change, many races have concluded under green that would have ended with the winner coasting to the checkered flag. And sometimes the two-lap restart resulted in a different winner, adding drama at the end when fans would have seen a ho-hum crawl.

But the change wasn't universally accepted by drivers and crew chiefs. As the saying goes, cautions breed cautions. And restarts are dangerous, especially at the restrictor-plate tracks of Daytona and Talladega. The field is bunched together, and it's much easier for cars to bang into each other while fighting for position at the end. But it's somewhat safer in the final 10 laps since it's a single-file restart instead of two-by-two.

Some crew chiefs don't like it because it's possible to run out of fuel if the event goes extra laps. Teams carefully calculate fuel consumption over the scheduled distance. It's pretty disappointing if you run out of gas while leading because the event goes overtime. Hey, that's the breaks. Many crew chiefs now take into account the possibility of a green-white-checkered finish that includes a few additional laps.

NASCAR officials often red flag the race and stop the cars on the track if it looks like the clean-up from an accident will take a while. If a wreck happens with three laps to go, but it's obvious the debris will take at least 10 pace laps to clear, NASCAR throws a red flag. The race resumes with one caution lap before the G-W-C to determine the winner.

This system isn't perfect by any means. You only get one shot at it. If a wreck happens on the first lap of the restart, the race is over. That's fair. NASCAR can't keep restarting a race over and over. Theoretically, this could continue for hours if a caution came out during every G-W-C restart. But at least the fans get a reasonable chance to see the event end under green.

The first time the rule was used in a Cup event came at Indianapolis on August 8, 2004, in the Brickyard 400, one of the biggest events of the year. The 160-lap race was extended to 161 laps after Brian Vickers crashed on Lap 156. The ensuing restart took place on Lap 160. It didn't change the outcome. Jeff Gordon led on the restart and stayed in front to win the race for the fourth time. But he earned his record win under race conditions.

Mark Martin wasn't so fortunate in the 2007 Daytona 500 when it had a G-W-C overtime finish. Martin was less than half a lap away from winning the event that has eluded him his entire career when Kevin Harvick edged

Martin at the line in the closest electronically timed finish in Daytona 500 history.

The final seconds of the race were controversial because NASCAR officials delayed throwing a yellow when cars were crashing behind the leaders. And that leads us to the next underrated rule on the list.

4. FREEZING THE FIELD ON A CAUTION

For more than five decades, NASCAR played its own version of Russian Roulette on the race track. It was known as racing back to the yellow. Whenever a caution came out, the drivers raced back to the start-finish line. Never mind the fact that wrecked cars and injured drivers could be in the way as they came back around to the flagstand.

That's not racing. It's Demolition Derby. The danger was enormous.

For years, drivers had a so-called "Gentleman's Agreement" not to race each other back to the yellow flag when a caution came out. It didn't always work that way. NASCAR chairman Brian France took that option away after a nasty wreck at Loudon, New Hampshire, when Dale Jarrett spun at the start/finish line with cars racing full speed around him.

The old rule also encouraged game playing. The leader would often deliberately let a driver get back on the lead lap (especially if he was a teammate) by slowing down just enough for them to pass him before he reached the line. That also made things exceedingly dangerous as drivers of the lapped cars zoomed past slower cars on the lead lap to try to get their lap back while hoping to avoid debris and crashed cars on the track.

NASCAR finally came to its senses in 2003 and adopted the rule most other racing leagues were using of freezing the field when the caution is displayed. Occasionally, that led to some confusion. NASCAR uses electronic scoring loops at several points around the track. A driver's position at the yellow was determined based on where he was as he passed the last scoring loop, not where he was at the moment of the caution.

In the large packs typically seen at Talladega and Daytona, positions are separated by inches at 190 mph, so resetting the field is challenging and sometimes a point of debate with the teams. It's a minor inconvenience considering the overall gain of safety for the competitors.

The gray area in this rule is when NASCAR officials decide to throw the caution. That led to a controversial moment at the end of the 2007 Daytona 500. On the final lap of an overtime Green-White-Checkered finish, Mark Martin and Kevin Harvick were fighting for the lead when several cars began crashing behind them in Turn 4.

Rather than throwing a caution and freezing the field at that point, NASCAR let the race continue, allowing Kevin Harvick to pass Martin before he crossed the finish line. Martin's many fans, hoping to finally see him win at Daytona, were furious. They believed NASCAR had swallowed the whistle, so to speak, breaking the rules of immediately calling the caution.

In this instance, NASCAR was right. They delayed the caution for two or three seconds, and the crashing cars were behind the two men battling for the biggest prize in the sport. It allowed the leaders to decide the finish under green and didn't compromise safety. Even if the yellow had flown two seconds sooner, it wouldn't have changed a thing in the wreck, but it would have ruined the finish.

NASCAR went old school for a moment, but the new rule of freezing the field under yellow has made stock car racing a much safer sport.

5. HALF WAY AND IT'S OVER

Many fans don't like this one, but it's a necessary rule to compensate for bad weather days. If an event completes half the laps, it can go in the books as a completed race. NASCAR officials want to do everything possible to complete a race on the day scheduled. On a rainy afternoon, that sometimes proves impossible.

The odds of getting a race into the books greatly increase if the event only needs to get to the halfway point. Obviously, fans want to see all the scheduled laps, but most of them don't want to come back on a Monday to do it. And none of the teams want to stay an extra day. It's costly, and it makes it more difficult to get to the next event. That problem is magnified if the next race is across the country or the next race is a Saturday night after a Sunday event the previous weekend.

Sometimes getting in half the laps is the only sensible thing to do. The teams all have weather radar screens on the pit wagon, so they know if rain is coming. They often adjust their strategy on fuel and tires based on when they think the race will end.

CHAPTER 5

Making Some New NASCAR Rules

If it isn't working, fix it. Traditionally, that isn't how NASCAR does things. Before making a major change, NASCAR often sends up a trial balloon to gauge the interest. Information about a possible change will leak out to the media. It gets written about and talked about for a few months, and NASCAR officials take a reading on the reaction before making a decision.

NASCAR has been slow to change throughout most of its history, but recent years have seen a rush to move forward. Some of those changes haven't been accepted by many of the traditional fans. The Chase playoff format, moving races from rural tracks in the Southeast to major markets out West, and the new Car of Tomorrow are three changes that the old-school fans find irritating.

All three have merit, however. The Chase has added excitement down the stretch by trying to keep the points championship up for grabs until the end of the season. Some fans called the Chase "The Kenseth Rule." In the final two months of the 2003 season, the last before the Chase playoff was implemented, Kenseth built an insurmountable points lead. The championship was a foregone conclusion by the start of October.

That wasn't unusual. Adding up the points for the entire season often meant one driver ran way with the title. The Chase haters say that's how it should be. The driver who dominates deserves to win the championship in a cakewalk. It's a fair argument, but it isn't the way other sports do it. For three consecutive years starting in 2002, the team that won the World Series did not win its division title. The wild-card entry won each year—the Anaheim Angels in 2002, the Florida Marlins in 2003, and the Boston Red Sox in 2004.

In an era of increased competition for the entertainment dollar, sports leagues have to build excitement toward the end of the season. Otherwise, fans stop buying tickets, stop watching on TV, and stop caring. NASCAR officials had that in mind when they went to the Chase for the Championship, and it also added drama for teams hoping to earn one of the 12 spots in the 10-race playoff.

It also brought more attention for sponsors because more cars were in contention late in the season. Sponsors are more important in NASCAR than any other sport, and many of the recent changes came with the sponsors in mind. NASCAR also realized its sponsors wanted more races in bigger markets and nicer facilities. So NASCAR came up with a realignment plan to spread out the schedule and take away races in the oversaturated Southeast.

Racing in Rockingham, North Carolina, doesn't have the same impact for sponsors as racing in the Los Angeles market. As I pointed out in the Speedways chapter, most primary sponsors have far more clients, employees, and stores in a major market like Los Angeles or Dallas than they would in a Rockingham or Martinsville.

NASCAR officials also realized they can't stand still and hope to progress as a mainstream sport. Increasing the fan base beyond the Southeast and into new areas is essential for continued growth, but it's a tricky proposition. The hard part is adding new fans with new ideas while trying to maintain the loyal long-time fans who want to keep things the way they were.

The one change that hasn't worked well was moving the Southern 500 from Darlington to California on Labor Day weekend, a move seen by many traditional fans as an insult to NASCAR history.

Every change hasn't turned out as well as NASCAR officials hoped, but in general, moving races to new places and bigger markets is the right thing to do. It's a trend that will continue. Staying on the farm, so to speak, isn't an option when sponsors are forking over $20 million a season to put their name on the hood of a car.

Then we have the Car of Tomorrow, a car that Tony Stewart once described as "the flying brick." The new car has issues. First, it's a little ugly, big and boxy, and not as sleek in styling as the old model. Second, it's harder to drive because it doesn't turn easily. Third, teams can't change much on it, so it's hard to make the car better.

At times, passing up front was almost impossible. Throughout the 2008 season, Cup teams were still trying to figure it out, but NASCAR wasn't inclined to help them with any adjustments. Time will probably take care of the competition issues. People need to remember that the No. 1 reason for going to the new car was safety.

The COT is vastly safer than the previous model. The steering wheel and driver's seat have been moved four inches to the right and away from the door panel. The door panels have increased structural support and foam padding. The car also has larger crush areas to reduce G-forces on impact. Safety issues alone are enough to make the changes worthwhile, but the fans and the competitors won't be happy until the car races better.

Most Overrated Theme
BACK TO BASICS

So many things changed over a five-year period that NASCAR officials felt it was time to step back a little. They entered the 2008 season with a theme of going back to basics. The idea was to gain back the trust of the traditional fans by slowing down on the changes and making it appear NASCAR was returning to its roots.

Talk about overrated. NASCAR has no real plans to turn back the clock and go back to racing at North Wilkesboro or some dirt track in South Carolina. It isn't going to do away with the Chase. It isn't going back to the old car. And NASCAR isn't going to stop moving to new markets, although that's on hold for the moment. International Speedway Corp. has found it difficult to build new facilities in Seattle, New York, and Denver.

ISC wants more than $200 million in public funding help. Not happening. Seattle couldn't get the finding to build a new facility for the Sonics and keep the team from moving to Oklahoma City. Getting state legislators to spend $200 million on a race track is a pipe dream.

Eventually, ISC will find a way to build in these markets, and older tracks will lose races—it's inevitable. The Dodgers used to play in Ebbets Field, and there are old-timers in Brooklyn still angry that they left. So the "back to basics" theme is a temporary halt to changes in NASCAR's growth pattern. But there are some trends within the sport that need some new rules.

Most Overrated Trend
CUP DRIVERS IN THE NATIONWIDE SERIES

NASCAR has managed to reduce the second most popular racing series in America to nothing more than a glorified practice round for Cup competitors, and it won't stay No. 2 for long (the newly merged IndyCar Series is gaining) if major changes aren't made soon.

Cup drivers won three consecutive Nationwide Series (formerly the Busch Series) championships from 2006 through 2008. That's a travesty— you might as well have Alex Rodriguez win the MVP award for Triple A baseball.

The sad part is that track promoters are all for it. Why? Money. They are convinced the Cup drivers are money in the bank.

Texas Motor Speedway president Eddie Gossage sent out a press release in the spring of 2008 emphasizing his strong feelings for keeping Cup stars in the Nationwide races. "The people of the Nationwide Series need to decide if they want to be the major league series they are now or go back to being a minor league series," Gossage said in the release.

Gossage is the best of the best at using spin to make his point. But the Nationwide Series isn't the major leagues—Sprint Cup holds down that spot. Gossage emphasized his point, "This Buschwhacking idea is way out of hand and uninformed," he said. "They act like this is a new thing. People forget that the winner of the first Busch Series race (1982 at Daytona) was Dale Earnhardt, two years after he won his first Cup championship."

That's true, but a tad misleading. Cup drivers have competed in the second-tier league since it started, but they weren't racing the full Nationwide schedule and competing for the series title. That first happened in 2006 when Kevin Harvick won the crown. Carl Edwards did it in 2007, the last title under the Busch beer banner. Nationwide Insurance took over in 2008.

The trend has continued for Cup stars and Cup teams to run rough-shod over the feeder-league regulars. Last time I checked, Arizona Diamondbacks pitcher Brandon Webb wasn't planning to make 30 starts for the Tucson farm club. Granted, the situation in NASCAR isn't the same. Cup drivers sell tickets to Nationwide events.

Gossage claims Cup drivers are the reason 100,000 people show up at Texas Motor Speedway for its Nationwide events, and the reason the speed-way can pay a $1.2 million purse for those races. "Otherwise, they may have to go back to 8,000-seat speedways and pay $100,000," Gossage said.

If Cup drivers never race in another Nationwide event, that won't happen, but we get the point. Speedways and purses have grown enor-mously. Cup drivers help fuel the monster and bring the attendance needed to make the Nationwide Series viable at major-market facilities.

Many Nationwide events on companion weekends (when the Cup race is the next day), however, have a field of almost half Cup drivers in cars pre-pared by Cup teams. What we're left with is a league without its own identity.

What's needed is a way to build up the Nationwide regulars and make them better known as they hone their skills. NASCAR officials have said they never want to tell a driver he can't compete in a lower-level event (be it Nationwide or the Trucks series) simply because he's a Cup racer.

So what's the answer?

New Rules
LIMITS ON CUP DRIVERS IN NATIONWIDE SERIES

During the 2007 season, NASCAR officials discussed a compromise plan. Cup drivers could continue to race in as many Nationwide events as they chose, but they would not earn points. Any driver ranked in the top 35 in Cup points cannot earns points in a Nationwide event. Only Nationwide regulars who aren't full-time Cup racers could compete for the Nationwide championship.

This would allow the Nationwide-only drivers and teams to receive much-needed recognition and financial incentives to produce increased involvement. Cup drivers have to compete in the Nationwide Series now for the league to have a full field each week. Only seven drivers competed full time for the final Busch title in 2007.

One problem caused the other. The increased participation of Cup teams made it impossible for Nationwide-only teams to compete in their own series because of the increased costs. Keeping the Cup regulars from racing for the Nationwide title seems reasonable. Give the up-and-coming drivers who don't compete in Cup a realistic chance to compete for the Nationwide championship.

That plan also has its detractors. Some say it would create a watered-down champion, a Nationwide regular who didn't run as well as a Cup driver who ran the full season in the feeder league. It's a strong possibility and a reason why NASCAR should limit the Cup drivers to 20 Nationwide events a year. Since that isn't likely, keeping them out of title contention is the next best option. Besides, is it more watered down than a Cup standout bullying his way to a title in a support league? At least the new plan would recognize the accomplishment of an up-and-coming driver trying to make a name for himself.

Some sponsors won't like this idea. Sponsors might balk at putting up the money to back a Cup regular in the Nationwide Series if they know going in he can't win the championship. But the Cup driver still goes to Victory Lane if he wins a race, so it shouldn't be a problem.

NEW RULE FOR THE TWO FEEDER LEAGUES: A CHASE PLAYOFF FOR THE NATIONWIDE SERIES AND THE TRUCK SERIES.

Why should the Cup guys have all the fun? NASCAR's other two touring leagues need a playoff similar to the Chase. Both would need to reduce the number of competitors from 12 to eight, but it would add excitement in the fall months. The Truck Series would also need a shorter playoff (probably eight events) since that series only runs 25 races a year.

The Nationwide Series would include only Nationwide regulars. No full-time Cup drivers would be eligible. This is the best thing NASCAR could do to build name recognition for the Nationwide drivers. It also would increase attendance down the stretch because fans would closely watch the eight drivers fighting for the title.

The Truck Series has enjoyed some close battles for the title in recent years, but it usually involves only two drivers. A Chase would increase the chances of several drivers vying for the championship at the end of the season.

NEW QUALIFYING RULE NO. 1: NO GUARANTEED SPOTS

Qualifying in its present form is the most overrated part of a race weekend. So stop giving teams a free ride in qualifying. You make your qualifying laps and take your chances—now there's a way to increase attendance on Friday afternoon.

Time to man up, boys. Get it done, or go home.

Now before all you Dale Earnhardt Jr., Jeff Gordon, or Tony Stewart fans throw a hissy fit, we'll agree to one tiny protection measure for your heroes. Fans don't want to pay good money only to find out their favorite driver isn't in the race, and TV networks definitely don't want that to happen. So give the top 30 in points a couple of Mulligan's a year (provisionals. as NASCAR calls them) for the rare spinout or engine problem on a qualifying lap.

And really, how often does that happen for the top drivers? About as often as they recite Shakespeare. If you use up your two insurance policies, too bad, because it's real competition for qualifying. Competing is the name of the game here, folks.

In the NHRA every drag racer shows up every week trying to make one of the top 16 spots, or goes home on Sunday. The best of the best, including the legendary John Force, have missed the show and packed up.

That's why they call it racing. What's fair about a driver in the top 35 taking a spot away from another driver who was 10 spots better in qualifying? It's not only overrated, it's un-American.

NEW QUALIFYING RULE NO. 2: POINTS FOR THE POLE

While we're at it, give a few points to the top qualifiers. Maybe five points for the pole, three for the No. 2 spot, and two for the third qualifier. Qualifying would become a meaningful event again and could have an impact on which drivers make the Chase.

This is a far better idea than awarding five points for leading a lap. As it is now, a driver gets zero points for a far more meaningful accomplishment than leading a lap under caution. Adding points for the pole would add a little drama to qualifying for the fans and make teams with guaranteed spots take it a little more seriously.

If a driver won five poles in the first 26 races, those additional 25 points could make the difference between making the Chase and falling short. And it's another way to increase fan interest. Do you really want to sell more tickets on Friday? That's how to do it.

NEW RULE NO. 1 FOR WINNING: WIN AND YOU'RE IN

As we've already pointed out, winning in NASCAR is vastly underrated. There's an easy solution for emphasizing victories in the regular season: Win and you're in. It's just that simple. If a driver wins one of the first 26 races, it earns him a spot in the Chase. That makes winning pretty darn important.

Obviously, a couple of restrictions are needed if that idea was adopted. A driver couldn't win the Daytona 500 to start the season and then skip all the races until the Chase begins. The win-and-you're-in plan only pays off if the driver remains in the top 20 in the standings, or maybe the top 25. A driver would still need to participate in the majority of the races and remain competitive.

This little addendum to the rules for making the Chase would give the smaller teams with limited funding a chance at making the playoff if they could find a way to win one event.

It would also give a big-name driver a chance to salvage a disappointing season. Dale Earnhardt Jr. didn't make the Chase in 2007, his last year at Dale Earnhardt, Inc. It was a tumultuous season when Earnhardt ultimately decided he needed to part ways from his step-mother (team owner Teresa Earnhardt) and the organization that bears his family name.

Earnhardt didn't win a race in 2007, but his legion of fans could have gone to the final regular season event at Richmond knowing he still had a chance to make the Chase if he could finish first on the Virginia short track, a place where he had won in the past.

It would be an enormous incentive for any winless driver in the top 25 heading to the final race before the playoff. Call it NASCAR's version of a wild card.

This idea is another way NASCAR could protect its stars. Jeff Gordon or Tony Stewart or Earnhardt might rank 13th in the standings, one spot outside the Chase cutoff. But they could still make it if they had won a race in the first six months of the season.

NEW RULE NO. 2 FOR WINNING: 50 ADDITIONAL POINTS FOR A VICTORY

If a driver and a team knew winning a race was worth 50 more points than it is now, things might get a lot more interesting at the end of each race. Teams would be tempted to go for it and take chances to try to earn the victory.

This could also add drama at the end of the season. If a driver is 45 points behind the leader entering the final race of the Chase, odds are he's not going to make up that difference unless the points leader wrecks or has a mechanical failure. All that changes if the victory is worth 50 additional points. The points leader can't play it safe if the guy right behind him in the standings has a chance to win.

NEW RULE NO. 1 TO STOP CHEATING: TOSS 'EM OUT

If NASCAR really wants to eliminate rule breakers, it's as easy as the old heave-ho. The only way to stop the cheaters is to kick them out of a race. Sit out an event and you'll get some real rehabilitation. It's a guaranteed cheat-stopper—if you can't play by the rules, you can't play.

Robin Pemberton, NASCAR's director of competition, said in 2007 that NASCAR isn't ready for that extreme form of punishment. "We haven't gotten there yet," Pemberton said. "The crew chiefs are the ones responsible for the people and their equipment. But we will keep elevating this when time comes to raise it up."

NASCAR has continued to raise the bar in its penal system. The Haas/CNC Racing team got the all-time whopper in 2008—150 points and $100,000 each for the No. 66 and No. 70 Chevrolets, along with a six-week suspension for the two crew chiefs. The crime? Deliberately moving the rear-wing mounts after a pre-race inspection.

Carl Edwards and the No. 99 Ford team got a big penalty at Las Vegas in 2008 (100 points and $100,000), plus the 10 bonus points Edwards would have received in the Chase for winning the race. They had a loose oil-tank lid, which is an aerodynamic advantage.

Will those severe penalties be enough? Not a chance. No matter how big the penalty, every team still races on Sunday. They didn't have the crew chief on the pit box, but that's like sending the manager to the showers in the ninth inning of a major league baseball game. It doesn't change much.

NASCAR suspended crew chief Chad Knaus before the 2006 Daytona 500, but his team and his driver (the No. 48 Chevy with Jimmie Johnson) still won the race. Knaus was also suspended for six races in 2007. Johnson won the championship both seasons. Well, that hurt, didn't it?

The deterrent isn't there, but the fear of missing a race would change the thought process for every team. Few teams would risk sitting one out, and only a team that feels it has little chance of making the field would risk cheating to try to get in. For the majority of teams, missing an event would have devastating consequences. Any contending team would severely damage its chances of making the Chase if it didn't compete in an event.

Carl Edwards drives his car during the NASCAR Sprint Cup Series UAW-Dodge 400 auto race at Las Vegas Motor Speedway on Sunday, March 2, 2008. (AP Photo/Jae C. Hong)

Try explaining that to the corporate sponsors who put up $20 million to place its company name on the hood. They'd probably want a rebate on their investment. Here's a conservative look at the math. If a company is paying $15 million a year as a primary sponsor, that's more than $400,000 per race. Talk about a fine that would get your attention.

Because the sponsors are the lifeblood of racing, they are a big reason NASCAR won't take such a drastic anti-cheating step. In 2007, NASCAR chairman Brian France said more than 100 Fortune 500 companies are involved in the sport. The corporate world invests hundreds of millions of dollars in NASCAR. Racing teams couldn't exist without them.

Mandating a punishment that would keep a sponsor off the track for a week isn't in NASCAR's best interest. Or is it? Isn't it better for the sport to appear free of impropriety? The sponsors would be sending the message, "We're here because NASCAR believes in integrity."

NASCAR officials could tell every team sponsor at the start of a season that if a team is caught with a flagrant violation of the rules, it will hold that team out of that race. A sponsor could write into a team's contract that a rebate was forthcoming if the team didn't compete in an event because of a NASCAR penalty.

But NASCAR has even bigger reasons for not telling a team it can't race—the fans. Imagine the negative reaction if Dale Earnhardt Jr. and the No. 88 Chevy were given a red card for the Daytona 500? Better call out the Florida National Guard on that one. Some of those 200,000 paying customers would ask for their money back. It all depends on whom NASCAR wants to send home. Sending J.J. Yeley home is no problem, if it's Tony Stewart, however, big problem.

Consequently, teams are willing to break the rules and take a chance because they can. They know NASCAR isn't going to throw them out. Take the situation in 2007 when the cars for Jeff Gordon and Jimmie Johnson had illegal body modifications that were found before the road race at Infineon Raceway. Neither team was allowed to practice or qualify. They were forced to start in the back for the Toyota/Save Mart 300 in cars capable of winning. NASCAR later announced both teams would receive the double-100 penalty of 100 points and $100,000. Both crew chiefs were suspended for six weeks. None of it mattered. Gordon entered the Sonoma race with a 264-point lead in the standings. Johnson was third, 73 points out of second place and 337 points behind Gordon. Both men were safely inside the 12-driver cutoff for the Chase playoff.

The teams gambled on something outside the rules. Why not? In the big picture, it wasn't much of a risk. The pain of getting caught was minimal. Until NASCAR is willing to park a car for a race, the circus game of "catch me if you can" will continue.

NASCAR officials say they aren't playing around and they mean business. They say they won't tolerate rule violators. But every time you think the teams are starting to get the message, they fool us again and drift back into the cheating mode—or trying to find the gray area, if you prefer.

Although the penalties from NASCAR keep escalating, these guys keep breaking the rules. It's like a teenager when mom says, "Don't come home late." It becomes a dare. The kid comes home late until the punishment exceeds the crime. None of that rhetoric matters. Sometimes, it takes getting grounded.

The 100-point penalty Gordon received was less than half of his lead in the standings. Johnson's penalty moved him from third to fourth. Gosh, that stings. None of it mattered because Chase drivers are seeded by victories.

Racing without their crew chiefs was also relatively painless. Hendrick Motorsports has the deepest talent pool in NASCAR with more than 500 employees. The crew chiefs weren't at the race track, but they were in the shop every day during the week—where they are needed the most—helping prepare cars for each race.

Six-figure fines have reached $150,000. For most of us, that's life-changing money. For Cup teams, it's like throwing a coin in the wishing well.

NASCAR has to make the punishment meaningful. For Gordon and Johnson in 2007, even sitting out a race wouldn't have been a major problem. It wouldn't have changed where either man finished at the end of the season. But missing a race would have been a huge embarrassment and a big loss of exposure for their sponsors. If the crews for the No. 24 and No. 48 cars thought missing the race was a possibility, do you think they would mess with the sheet metal, flare out those fenders, and hope nobody noticed? Of course not.

When the risk becomes greater than the reward, the incentive to gamble doesn't look so appealing. What's missing here is fear. So far, no one is scared straight.

Most Overrated NASCAR Policy
SUBSTANCE ABUSE CONTROL

NASCAR received a gigantic wake-up call in April 2008 when Aaron Fike admitted in an *ESPN The Magazine* story that he was injecting heroin while competing in Craftsman Truck Series events. It was a clear warning to NASCAR officials to end its archaic and failed drug-testing policy before it was too late. In the case of Fike and the people who raced alongside him, it already was too late.

That situation should have proved to NASCAR that its 20-year policy of "reasonable suspicion" for drug testing does not work. A month after Fike's admission, NASCAR chairman Brian France said the sanctioning body would review its substance-abuse policy and determine if changes were needed.

Changes will take place in 2009, but they should have happened long ago. The "reasonable suspicion" plan was nothing more than Russian Roulette on a racetrack, a hope that you guessed right and caught the driver who could endanger the entire field. Fike's admission was the long-feared scenario of a driver racing a car at 200 mph while impaired by substance abuse. Odds are it has happened far more often than we know because NASCAR didn't have a detailed testing plan in place to prevent it.

NASCAR was woefully behind the curve on this issue compared to other major sports leagues when it should have been the leader in controlling substance abuse. Unlike other sports, the abuser isn't just endangering himself. A driver under the influence of drugs is endangering the entire field, because he is attempting to control a 3,400-pound weapon that is capable of killing himself and the other drivers on the track.

NASCAR spokesman Jim Hunter said no system is perfect, and he's 100 percent right. The black cloud of steroid abuse that continues to haunt baseball is proof positive. But NASCAR's failure to test every driver on a regular basis is impossible to justify. Seven NASCAR drivers were suspended for substance abuse from 2001 through 2008. Three of those were caught by law enforcement officers.

So NASCAR caught four drivers in eight years. Four in eight years? That can only mean one thing: Others probably weren't caught because they weren't tested. It's unrealistic to believe in today's society that such a small number of competitors would test positive.

All NASCAR drivers sign a form at the beginning of the season that states they can be randomly drug tested at any time. The problem is it rarely happens. One week after Fike's admission, most Cup drivers said they had never undergone a drug test as NASCAR competitors. "In the 10 years that I've raced, I've never been drug-tested," Kevin Harvick said. "To me, that's not a proper drug policy for a professional sport. We haven't made any headway whatsoever on the drug-testing policy."

NASCAR's substance-abuse policy includes the right to test any driver at any time, but officials only do so if they believe a competitor might have a problem. If the system worked so well, how did they strike out on Fike?

Cup driver Kasey Kahne said he had suspicions about Fike. "I definitely wondered about Aaron, so I'm sure others did," Kahne said. "When he said he did heroin before a race, that's incredible that no one knew. As much money as there is in this sport, I think we should take a little more effort to make sure every driver is clean."

Harvick believes NASCAR should have changed its substance-abuse policy long ago. "You can tell I'm a little bit frustrated about the situation," he said. "As someone who respects the sport and respects my sponsors, I'm upset that I have to answer questions about Aaron Fike. It really ticks me off, because every driver in this garage should be taking random drug tests."

NASCAR officials were on the defensive after Fike's story was published. "The responsibility here rests across the board—with the drivers and competitors, owners, teams and NASCAR," said Kerry Tharp, NASCAR's director of communication, the week after Fike's actions were revealed. "We test an individual when we have reasonable suspicion. A positive test results in severe consequences and is a career-changing moment for that person.

"NASCAR's policy is also supported by the various policies that the teams have in place that are required under the driver/owner agreements. No system is flawless, but we believe our zero tolerant policy that is in place has served the sport well." How do you know without testing? The worst-case scenario is that backroom deals were negotiated. What if drivers did test positive but were given a slap on the wrist and privately told to clean up or face the consequences?

The irony of this is that NASCAR does a far better job of testing rule violations on the cars than it does the drivers. Every race car goes through meticulous inspections at every race. Fractions of an inch can bring major fines, points reductions, and suspensions for crew members. NASCAR only tests someone if it feels that driver may have a problem. How many parents across America could testify how hopelessly naïve that concept is?

NASCAR officials said in 2005 that 40 to 45 drug tests were administered during the previous two seasons—20 to 25 tests in a year would mean about half the drivers were tested if you only included Sprint Cup. Such a limited testing plan has no realistic chance of finding competitors with substance-abuse problems.

It was 1988 when the late Bill France Jr. announced that NASCAR would test drivers based on reasonable suspicion. They got away with it for 20 years because the vast majority of competitors in this sport are clean. Those who aren't need to be removed. Since Dale Earnhardt's death in 2001, NASCAR has done a remarkable job of improving the safety of racing. Testing drivers on a hunch doesn't qualify as an acceptable way to keep competitors safe.

New Rule Finally in Place for 2009
RANDOM DRUG TESTING

No trial balloon is needed on this one. Almost everyone involved in NASCAR believes this change should have happened years ago. Drivers should undergo random drug testing several times a year. That policy should also include crew members who jump in front of moving vehicles and risk injury every week.

In September 2008, NASCAR announced it will implement random drugs tests throughout the year beginning in 2009, along with mandatory testing for all drivers and crew members before the season begins. Teams from every series must verify that all licensed crew members have been tested by a certified lab prior to the season. The plan calls for drivers to undergo random drug testing several times a year, with tests conducted at each event.

Kevin Harvick and his wife, DeLana, own Truck Series and Nationwide Series teams at Kevin Harvick Inc. Fike drove for them briefly, but Harvick said he didn't test his employees at that time. He changed that policy a few weeks after Fike's admission, adding random drug testing at KHI.

Fike was arrested for possession of heroin in July 2007 while in his car at an amusement park. Drivers voiced their concerns then. "Shame on NASCAR for not policing our garage better than they police it right now," Harvick said. "I think we're all professional athletes and should be treated like professional athletes in other professional sports—and shame on them for not doing that." In support of regular testing, Jeff Burton said, "There's too much at stake for this sport, too much at stake for the drivers, the race-track and the crew members on pit road."

Most Cup drivers have said they are in favor of regular testing. A week after Fike admitted using heroin while racing, not a single driver had a problem with random drug testing. "I would love it," Tony Stewart said. "I've never been asked to take one yet. I think it should be mandatory. I think it's a great idea. The Fike situation shows that as an organization, we're not doing a good job of seeing this before it happens."

The fear of being on the track with someone who has a drug problem made any inconvenience of a random drug test seem insignificant. "I'm sure I'll have to do it for speaking my mind," Harvick said. "But if I have to pee in a cup 15 times a year, I'm happy to do it.

"The bad part is it isn't fair to the 95 percent of this garage that is clean. But I want everybody in the world to know our sport is clean. I want fans and sponsors to know this garage is clean."

Racing cars is dangerous enough without the additional risk of racing against someone on drugs. "I have been in a race with [Fike], and I know for a fact that he's not the only one," Harvick said. "There's another driver that was suspended that I can almost guarantee you was in the race car while he was under the influence, and that pisses me off. I'm sure I'll be blasted for saying what I feel, but I don't want to be on a race track with people like that. It's irresponsible more than anything."

NASCAR and its fans face a possible dilemma with regular testing for all the drivers. What if one of the stars of the sport faced suspension in the middle of a season or at the start of the Chase? It's a more costly penalty than football and baseball teams have if an athlete is suspended. Even a short suspension would mean a driver's championship hopes were over; not just for him, but for his entire team and his sponsors.

It's also a problem for the fans of that driver. They spend hard-earned money on tickets and travel expenses to see him race, but any sensible fan would realize something has to be done. The possible consequences of ignoring the problem far outweigh the fan disappointment or the loss for a team and its sponsors.

"I had a long talk with NASCAR about this [in 2007]," Harvick said. "It almost seems like it fell on deaf ears. They were more mad that I had a reaction to the situation than they were about trying to move forward."

Tharp said NASCAR officials always take it seriously when drivers come to them with questions or complaints. "Let me assure you that no issue or conversation that we have with a driver, owner or team member ever falls on deaf ears," Tharp said. "Now, they might not always come out of the meeting with the answer they're looking for, but we listen."

Jimmie Johnson is glad NASCAR listened to the drivers about changing its policy. "I've not been tested before," Johnson said. "But I'm confident every driver is willing to do whatever it takes."

Harvick said he thought NASCAR needed to do a better job of staying ahead of the curve. "It's just like the safety thing back in 2001," he said. "We didn't react until that situation happened [with Dale Earnhardt's death]. With drug-testing, there's no reason in the world today not to be proactive. This is about forward thinking about how the drivers are perceived from a public standpoint. If I'm a fan, I don't want to think, 'Are they really clean?' This always has been perceived as a clean sport. Let's not let that change now, because it is. But let's prove it."

NASCAR has been forced to do the right thing and move forward to ensure that the sport is clean, even if it means suspending a top driver in the middle of a season. However, even with the new random testing plan, the system has a potential flaw: NASCAR doesn't list which substances would bring an automatic ban. That leaves an unnecessary gray area and will open up NASCAR to criticism and possible legal action.

NASCAR's new policy was announced two weeks after *ESPN The Magazine* revealed that Truck Series racer Ron Hornaday had taken steroids for two seasons because of a thyroid condition—but Hornaday never informed NASCAR officials he was taking the drug. Hornaday was cleared by NASCAR, but what happens if another driver tests positive for a steroid and doesn't have a legitimate medical reason for using it?

No particular drug is listed as banned. So NASCAR still has the option to clear anyone it wants after the test results are revealed or suspend anyone it wants based on any substance it deems a problem. Lawyers will line up to go to court over that situation.

Overrated Restart Rule
ALLOWING CARS TO START IN THE FRONT OF THE LEADER

NASCAR needs to stop allowing drivers on the tail end of the lead lap to line up in front of the leader on a restart. This happens occasionally, depending on when the caution drops and when drivers come to pit road.

It happened once in the February Cup race at Auto Club Speedway. Leader Matt Kenseth had eight cars in front of him on a restart at Lap 60.

This isn't fair to the driver leading the race. Let the tail-end cars go around and start in the back of the pack. It gives them almost a full lap for free, but it's better (and safer) than potentially slower cars starting in front of the leader.

CHAPTER 6

Bad Ideas, Misconceptions, Tough Talk, and One-Liners to Remember

NASCAR is filled with tough talk and braggadocio. Big money and big speed go hand-in-hand, so having a little bit of a cocky side to your personality is almost a requirement. But sometimes emotions get the best of NASCAR folks. They just can't help themselves, whether it's an owner protecting his turf or a fan losing his wits.

A lot of things are done on impulse—not always the best way to handle a difficult situation. Instinct can be a good thing, but it has a dark side. Occasionally, it's better to take a step back and realize that what you thought was the right thing at the time wasn't such a great idea.

A few of those issues are addressed in this chapter. I also list some misconceptions about the way NASCAR fans and competitors view some key points, including teammates, a lack of technology, and a warped view of the past.

Let's delve into some interesting items that deserve analysis from another point of view.

Most Underrated Paranoia
JACK ROUSH'S FEAR OF TOYOTA

No one has been a bigger critic of Toyota's entry into Cup racing that team owner Jack Roush, co-owner of Roush Fenway Racing, Ford's top team. And it sure is fun to hear Jack go off on one of his Toyota rants. Roush sounded like he was ready for a Don King production back in January 2007 on the eve of Toyota's first Cup season. Roush was ready to rumble, saying he was "going to war" and he planned to "hand Toyota their heads."

Wow! Put it on Pay-Per-View. A fender-to-fender splendiferous racing extravaganza, as the wild-haired master might say. It was the woe-is-me Roush Fords against the money-mad Toyota foreigners.

I expected Roush's trademark Panama hat to start spinning every time a Toyota question was asked during the media tour festivities at Roush's head-quarters. "We will not be intimidated by any new team or manufacturer that comes in," Roush said. "Toyota will not find that established teams will wither in their path as they have seen elsewhere. We're going to war with them, and they should give us their best shot."

On an "Outside the Lines" segment on ESPN, Roush was asked why he was scared of Toyota. "Did I say I was scared?" Roush barked. "I don't back away from a good fight. But Toyota could bring about changes in the way we conduct our business. About 90 percent of funding for Cup racing comes from sponsors and 10 percent from the manufacturers. If Toyota is funding 50 percent on its teams, that could upset the financial equilibrium of NASCAR and cause chaos."

Toyota officials got a good laugh out of that accusation. "It's ridiculous," said Jim Aust, Toyota's vice president of racing. "I think people at Roush Racing are saying these things to get more money out of their manufac-turer."

Roush was convinced then and still believes that NASCAR is headed down the road to ruin because Toyota is the evil empire with endless cash.

Jack Roush is no fan of Toyota. (AP Photo/Bob Brodbeck)

"They will try to outspend everyone and place the rest of us in a catch-up scenario," Roush said.

Roush wasn't alone among the Ford contingent in his Toyota hatred. Dan Davis, Ford's former director of racing, previously called Toyota "a predator." Both men said they believed Toyota was outbidding other man-ufacturers for top talent—engineers, fabricators, crew chiefs, drivers, etc.

Isn't this the normal way things work in a capitalist society? Business leaders go after the best people in hopes of producing a better product than their competitors. That's what the good-old USA is all about, however, the underlying feeling among some NASCAR followers that supporting Toyota is an un-American thing to do continues.

Toyota isn't just passing through. The auto manufacturer employs nearly 150,000 people in the United States. But it is a Japanese company and one of the world's most successful corporations at a time when American auto manufacturers are suffering. One could argue the U.S. auto industry did this to itself. If the American automakers had built more competitive passenger cars over the last 20 years, they wouldn't be in the financial turmoil they are today. That's a very debatable idea, but it's not the point here.

Ford officials are complaining the loudest against Toyota. GM and Dodge officials haven't followed the constant, angry diatribe about Toyota that comes from Roush and the Ford camp. Rick Hendrick, who owns Chevrolet's top NASCAR team, doesn't have a problem competing with Toyota. "I think it's good for the sport to have another manufacturer involved," Hendrick said before the 2007 season. "But it's NASCAR's job to maintain the equal playing field."

Midway through the 2008 season, some people weren't so sure NASCAR kept its end of the bargain. Toyota led the standings with Kyle Busch at Joe Gibbs Racing, which was dominating Cup. The Camry engines had more horsepower that the other manufacturers. Why? Toyota officials did their homework, signed a top team, and got a lot better after a horrible inaugural season in 2007.

Was the drastic turnaround a sign of things to come? Speedway Motorsports Inc. mogul Bruton Smith predicted in 2007 that Toyota would be a force in NASCAR at the Cup level. Smith owns Toyota dealerships and has a firsthand look at Toyota's money machine. "Toyota is an extremely wealthy company," Smith said. "I don't think it's bad, but it's something that is going to change the sport over a period of years. We live in a democracy, and that's how it is. If they want to buy their way to a championship, they have the money to do it."

Buying a championship isn't as easy as it sounds. It is estimated that Toyota is spending more than $400 million a year in Formula One, but it hasn't come close to competing for the constructor's title. NASCAR is a much different animal, one that Toyota easily tamed in the Craftsman Truck Series. In 2006, Toyota's third truck season, it placed seven drivers in the top 10 (including the top six) and won the championship with Todd Bodine.

Roush saw that and knew Toyota was coming to get him in Cup. But Roush's problem is that he's getting a taste of his own medicine. Teams like Roush Fenway Racing and Hendrick Motorsports, multicar operations with hundreds of employees and enormous budgets, made it impossible for the little guys like Wood Brothers and Petty Enterprises to compete.

Roush and Hendrick changed the business model, something Roush accused Toyota of doing. Ford was down to eight cars in 2008 for the Cup Series, and Roush Fenway was its only competitive team. Ford and Roush feel the biggest threat from Toyota, so they scream the loudest.

Roush was once asked by *Charlotte Observer* reporter David Poole, "If you were starting over today, wouldn't you try to hire the best people? Wouldn't you use all his resources to try to be competitive?" Roush talked about how he did it when he started in 1988: "I identified people that I thought had the skill sets and judgment to help me make the right decisions in NASCAR racing."

Isn't that what Toyota did? But Roush didn't let up. More than a year later in Atlanta, he let the vitriol fly again after his old pal Lee White, Toyota's GM of Racing, took a shot back. Roush was livid at the Atlanta race in March of 2008 after learning White accused Roush Fenway Racing of deliberately cheating in a *USA Today* article earlier that week.

Most Underrated One-Liner
ROUSH CALLING WHITE "AN ANKLE-BITING CHIHUAHUA"

You gotta love that one. It was the latest salvo in one sweet feud that may never go away.

This paranoia about Toyota goes deeper than one little man with a Napoleon complex. Roush is willing to publicly rag on Toyota at every opportunity, but he isn't alone.

When the Camrys were the fastest cars in 2008 preseason testing, the competing teams howled. You would have thought a Congressional investigation was in order. Some fans love that Roush picks on Toyota. Even a driver or two has chimed in. It was Jimmy Spencer who once said, "You know those guys bombed Pearl Harbor."

There's a portion of the NASCAR fan base that will never accept a foreign manufacturer, a racing version of xenophobia. But Toyota isn't leaving, and you can't turn back the clock. NASCAR also isn't going to bring a Cup race back to Rockingham or North Wilkesboro or Hickory or any other Carolina track from the past. Not next year, not ever.

White and Toyota became Roush's latest enemy. They should take it in stride. For more than 20 years, Roush has felt everyone in NASCAR is out to get him. If Roush isn't complaining, he isn't breathing. When his Car of Tomorrow entries weren't competitive in early 2007, Roush's excuse was he followed testing rules while the other teams didn't.

Roush was back to blasting NASCAR early in 2008 after Carl Edwards, Roush's rising star, was penalized 100 points for an oil-tank cover violation after winning at Las Vegas. That incident caused White to chime in and gave his opinion, which was more than Roush could stomach. White was due a free shot since Roush had criticized Toyota for more than a year.

Toyota did what it had to do to become competitive by signing Joe Gibbs Racing, one of the best teams in NASCAR. But Toyota's success brought more cries about the evil empire from across the ocean. Roush continued his soap-box rant, even accusing Michael Waltrip's Toyota team of deliberating stealing one of Roush Fenway's sway bars. Sure, a Roush sway bar is the reason for all of Toyota's success. Those dirty thieves.

Not exactly something he needs to take before the Supreme Court, but his feeling about the Toyota boys sure is entertaining.

Other Underrated Quotes
2. LOST IN TRANSLATION?

Donnie Wingo, the first Cup crew chief for Juan Pablo Montoya in the No. 42 Dodge, is a proud Southern boy from South Carolina. Montoya, who is Colombian, speaks fluent English, but English from someone who grew up in the Deep South is a little different. Wingo was asked if he had any communication problems with Montoya, "No, Juan says four-letter words just as good as any of us."

3. F1 BOREDOM

Montoya, who raced in Formula One before coming to NASCAR, was asked what advantages NASCAR racing has over Formula One. "Well, for one thing, here you might make 70 passes in one race," Montoya said. "In five and a half years of Formula One, I don't think I passed 70 cars total."

4. ALMOST ANYTHING FROM TONY STEWART WHEN HE FEELS SURLY

No one comes close to Stewart when he's in one of his condescending moods, which is most of the time. In 2007, Stewart was called to a meeting with NASCAR officials in the Nextel Cup hauler after he inferred on his radio show that races were rigged. Stewart and teammate Denny Hamlin also had a meeting with Joe Gibbs to discuss an on-track incident that had the Gibbs drivers criticizing each other.

So Stewart was asked this question: What has more impact, a meeting with Gibbs or a meeting in the NASCAR hauler? "Having to deal with guys like you [who] ask stupid questions like that," Stewart said. "That's worse than either of those two things."

Stewart was also asked what makes Indianapolis Motor Speedway so special. "You're kidding, right?" Stewart asked. "You don't know the answer to that? Do you want me to find somebody to tell you real quick so we can go on with stuff that people don't know the answer to yet? If they don't know that by now, they won't figure it out."

That's Tony at his best.

Most Overrated Fans
TALLADEGA

I'll give 'em one thing—they've got passion, misplaced as it may be.

In 2007, Tony Stewart compared NASCAR in-race decisions to professional wrestling, an opinion he later retracted after a come-to-Jesus meeting with the NASCAR bigwigs before a race at Talladega. Appropriate that the meeting took place at Talladega, the closest NASCAR has to wrestling fans. Actually, some folks in the stands there come closer to European soccer hooligans.

Cup victory No. 77 for Jeff Gordon was the moment he passed the legendary Dale Earnhardt on the career list for Cup wins. Unfortunately for Gordon, it came at the place where Earnhardt reached the status of a racing deity. The worst-case scenario for most of the Talladega fans came true. Gordon moved one spot ahead of their hero on what would have been Earnhardt's 56th birthday.

A few Neanderthals among the crowd of 170,000 decided to practice the shot put with beer cans. The cans took flight, whistling through the air as they sailed over the catch fence before crashing down on the track.

Beverage containers fly toward the car of Jeff Gordon as he drives out of turn four at the Talladega Superspeedway in Talladega, Alabama, on Sunday, April 25, 2004. Gordon had just won the NASCAR Aaron's 499 race under caution and many fans thought that rival NASCAR driver Dale Earnhardt Jr., had been leading when the caution came out with five laps remaining. (AP Photo/Phil Manson)

Comedian Jeff Foxworthy was the grand marshal that day. He should have trotted back out after the race, grabbed a microphone and added to his famous list: "If you hate the winner and throw your beer on the track, you might be a redneck."

This was not an isolated incident. The Dega rowdies had a worse display of idiocy in 2004 when Jeff Gordon defeated Earnhardt Jr. in a controversial yellow-flag finish. That day, some of the Talladega fans did their best to play the stereotypical part of drunken hillbilly fans. People threw anything they could get their hands on, including coolers filled with ice and beer.

It all started with NASCAR's decision to finish the race under caution instead of running a two-lap shootout. With four laps to go, Brian Vickers spun, bringing out the caution flag. NASCAR officials should have thrown the red flag and tried to finish with a green-white-checkered but decided it was a bad idea at a restrictor-plate track.

The decision cost Earnhardt Jr. a chance at his fifth Talladega victory in a span of six races on the 2.66-mile oval. NASCAR might as well have slapped Santa Claus or called Robert E. Lee a coward. Debris rained down on the track like a beer-can version of a ticker-tape parade. "They were just expressing themselves in the only manner that they saw fit," Earnhardt said at the time, comments he later regretted.

Talladega Superspeedway officials gave stern warnings at the events that came after that incident, but it didn't stop a few cavemen from firing away during Gordon's 2007 victory.

Gordon would have received boos almost anywhere when he passed Earnhardt's win total. The night he tied Earnhardt with a win at Phoenix, Gordon showed respect and class by holding a No. 3 flag on his victory lap. But it still brought a chorus of boos from the crowd, along with a couple of paper cups tossed on the track. But the post-race barrage of beer cans was an inexcusable display of ignorance.

To their credit, NASCAR and Talladega took it seriously to try to elim-inate this type of dangerous and moronic behavior in the future. Anyone caught doing it would be immediately thrown out and banned from the facility. Unfortunately, there's only so much you can do. Many speedway officials feel a few bad apples make an overall decent crowd look bad. "We have over a million people come to races at Texas Motor Speedway each year," TMS president Eddie Gossage said in 2007. "But we have fewer arrests in a year than the Dallas Cowboys have in one game."

Talladega fans aren't alone in bad behavior. Fans showered the Daytona asphalt with debris at the end of the 2002 Pepsi 400 when Michael Waltrip won under caution. And other sports have seen far worse. Cleveland Browns fans in the 1980s were notorious for throwing things at opposing players, including big chunks of ice, from the end-zone area known as "The Dawg Pound."

The difference for auto racing is the increased danger of hitting a moving race car. What if some Bozo tossed a full beer on the track during a race? The possible consequences of a can hitting the windshield of a car traveling close to 200 mph are unthinkable. That's tough to police. Tracks need a lot more security at massive grandstands like Talladega. Even 1,000 police officers is a tiny number compared to 170,000 fans.

Banning a violator isn't enough. The guilty party could still get in if someone else purchased the ticket. The track would need to check IDs at the gate, not a reasonable plan for a crowd of more than 100,000. But make it clear that arrests would be mandatory if a person was caught. "We can encourage local and state officials to increase the seriousness of the offense," Gossage said. "Instead of a misdemeanor, maybe this should be a felony."

Charging someone with disorderly conduct is not enough. The charge should be assault. A full beer can thrown in the air could easily injure another fan or a driver. Also, speedways could stop allowing fans to bring canned drinks into the facility, but that's a big selling point at some tracks. It's safer for everyone to buy a drink at a concession stand and have it poured into a plastic cup.

A full beer can is a dangerous weapon, but so is a shoe or a battery or a scanner. There's always something to throw if you're crazy enough to try, and Talladega has too many fans that are willing to risk it.

Gordon knew it was coming again at the virtual Earnhardt shrine, the place where The Intimidator won 10 times for the fans who worshiped him. "It's tough," Gordon said. "I knew three-quarters of these fans were against me. I didn't want to start a riot today, but I wanted to break that record."

He had to do it under caution when an accident happened after the green-white-checkered restart. No doubt the Talladega conspiracy theorists questioned the call before showing their anger.

"If NASCAR ever wanted to fix a race, you would think they would lean toward the majority," Gordon said. "I love the passion of the fans, but you have to use common sense." Gordon then drove to Victory Lane as quickly as he could to avoid the barrage. Hendrick Motorsports teammate Jimmie Johnson was tired of seeing it.

"It's terrible," Johnson said. "They are going to hurt someone. I'm sure some cans don't make it on the track. They could hit a kid in the back of the head. That's not a way to show you support our sport. I don't know the logic behind it. I just hope it goes away."

In fairness, the vast majority of the crowd behaved themselves. Track president Grant Lynch told the fans before the race that anyone throwing debris on the track would be arrested. Some of the folks who didn't listen, or didn't care, were handcuffed and escorted out by police officers while Gordon and his team celebrated in Victory Lane.

The majority of Talladega spectators were hoping to see Earnhardt Jr. win on his father's birthday. Junior settled for seventh on a day when he knew his No. 8 Chevy wasn't a winning ride. Earnhardt had no problem with Gordon passing his father on the win list. Two days before the race, Earnhardt said he hoped fans wouldn't react angrily if Gordon won, and if they had to throw something, throw toilet paper. A few rolls came down, but beer cans were the weapon of the moment.

Talladega is known for its sea of Confederate flags on the campgrounds and its wild infield debauchery where people travel at their own risk. That's more legend than fact. Track officials have worked hard in recent years to give the infield and campground environments more of a family atmosphere. But a Jeff Gordon victory sure can bring out a backwoods version of Mr. Hyde among the Dega nation.

Most Overrated Concept in NASCAR
TEAMMATES

Back in 2005, Mark Martin told me something that surprised me at first until I started to think about it. We were discussing his season when I asked him about a driver who was one of his teammates at the time. "Wait a minute," Martin said. "I don't have teammates. I have fellow drivers that race for the same team owner I do."

Point taken. The relationship of teammates in racing is different from any other sport. A NASCAR driver has to align himself with a strong multi-car team if he hopes to win consistently in this era. More cars mean more information to share and more ways to figure out things on the track.

The only real teammates a driver has are his pit crew and the guys who work on his cars at the shop. Another driver who races for the same team owner is more of a business associate. NASCAR is much different from stick-and-ball sports where the team concept is simple: If I win, you win. It doesn't work that way in racing. Drivers in the same organization usually try to help each other as much as they can. But everyone is trying to win the same thing, and only one driver earns it. Consequently, being a teammate only goes so far.

The NASCAR teammate relationship gets tested on the track at times. One good example was a 2007 race on the short track at Martinsville, Virginia, when Jeff Gordon was trying to pass Jimmie Johnson to win the Goody's Cool Orange 500. Gordon felt he had the fastest car that day, so he expected Johnson to give him some leeway. Forget that, teammate or no teammate, when drivers are racing for the victory in the final laps.

Teammate cooperation changes depending on the situation. Had it been Lap 50 and Gordon needed to lead a lap to earn the five bonus points, Johnson might have obliged. That's being a good teammate. But helpful gestures during a race are always subject to change. From the driver's perspective, here's the thought process: "If helping you doesn't hurt me, I'm happy to do it. If helping you might hinder my chances of winning...well, sorry pal, you're on your own."

This plays out constantly during a restrictor-plate race. Drivers talk about helping each other in the draft at Daytona and Talladega. A driver can't win a race at either track without help. Lining up with a teammate can help get a driver to the front. But it doesn't always work that way. If a teammate gets shuffled out of line, a driver isn't going to jump in behind him just because they're teammates. You work with your teammate if you can, but not to the detriment of your own chances of winning the event.

Martin's comment about teammates came in a year when Roush Racing had all five of its cars in the Chase. Some people thought the team had an advantage since half of the 10 championship contenders were Roush drivers.

Tony Stewart, who didn't have a teammate in the Chase, won the title, finishing 35 points ahead of Roush drivers Greg Biffle and Carl Edwards. Stewart had two teammates outside the Chase in Bobby Labonte and Denny Hamlin. They had nothing to lose. Their crew chiefs could pass along info to Greg Zipadelli, Stewart's crew chief, if they found something useful in practice.

But all five Roush drivers were trying to win the title. At some point, sharing information isn't in the best interest of a driver who wants to win.

Gordon's runner-up finish to Johnson at Martinsville came after Johnson's crew chief, Chad Knaus, asked for help from Steve Letarte, Gordon's crew chief. Letarte gave Knaus the set-up notes on Gordon's car. Knaus was quick to point out the situation has also happened the other way around with Knaus helping Letarte on Gordon's set-up.

The two men insisted that cooperative effort never changed while Gordon and Johnson battled for the championship in the final weeks of the Chase. But they weren't doing each other any favors once the races started. Letting your teammate pass to lead a lap and earn five bonus points wasn't an option.

In this case, the situation goes further than just teammates. The two men are close friends. Gordon has been a mentor to Johnson. He helped convince team owner Rick Hendrick to put Johnson in a Cup car. Gordon is also the co-owner of Johnson's No. 48 Chevy. When the championship was on the line late in the Chase, none of that mattered.

Gordon said he didn't want to wreck Johnson to win the race at Martinsville, although he gave Johnson a few teeth-rattling bumps to try to get by him. Had an identical situation come up during the Chase, Johnson probably would have found himself spinning and sliding into the wall.

You need teammates to win consistently in Cup, but there's only one winner each week and only one champion at the end. Sometimes a teammate is the guy you have to beat.

Most Overrated Dashboard Instrument
A TACHOMETER
Most Underrated Dashboard Instrument
A SPEEDOMETER

One solves the problem that the other one causes, so I put these two together. It's easy to be underrated if no car has one, which is the case in NASCAR. But adding one sure could end some penalties on pit road.

The tach is overrated because it's a poor substitute for judging exact speed in the race car, something every driver has to estimate when entering and leaving pit road. Since NASCAR was switching to the Car or Tomorrow full time in 2008, was it too difficult to add a simple speedometer from the Car of Yesteryear?

Many drivers and crew chiefs say they don't need it. If it's so unnecessary, why do so many drivers get caught speeding on pit road? Here's how bad it can get: At the Atlanta spring race in 2008, Dale Jarrett got caught speeding down pit road when he was coming in on a pass-through penalty for speeding on pit road.

All the cars have tachometers to show engine RPMs, but it must not be a truly accurate way to gauge speed when NASCAR officials are penalizing drivers for going a few miles per hour over the pit speed limit. Ever notice how much a tach gauge shoots up when you mash the gas quickly, even if you are in neutral?

Speedometers can also be inaccurate if not calibrated properly. NASCAR officials don't want to add that to the list of things they have to approve each week. So don't do it. Let the teams worry about it. If the speedometer is off, that's their problem. Something needs to change, because the current system of using the tach just isn't working.

Most Overrated Memories
RACES WERE BETTER BACK IN THE DAY

No Grandpa, it's time to wake up. Races weren't better in the old days. NASCAR officials have heard plenty of criticism in recent years about the lack of passing up front and the problems of not enough side-by-side racing in the Car of Tomorrow.

After a particularly boring race at Chicagoland Speedway in 2007 (still in the old car design), NASCAR sent out a statistical package to show how wrong it is to look back fondly on the racing of yesteryear. For example, from 1970 through 1994, there were 128 races in which the winner of the event was the only car on the lead lap, including 110 times in the 1970s.

Take a wild guess how many times that has happened from 1995 through 2007. Zero.

Officially, the 10 closest finishes in NASCAR history happened from the mid-1990s forward, including three of the top four in the past four years. However, they didn't have electronic timing in the old days, so that's a little misleading.

It's no stretch to say that racing today is better than it was 30 years ago. That's a fact. Even so, NASCAR still has Cup races that bore us to tears. The June race at Dover, Delaware, was the yawner of 2008. In 400 laps around the Monster Mile, Carl Edwards made the only on-track pass for the top spot, moving by Roush Fenway teammate Greg Biffle on lap 171.

Only six cars finished on the lead lap, and those six drivers weren't exactly racing for position at the end. Each of them was about four seconds apart. At least they were on the same lap, which often didn't happen 25 years ago. All sports have boring events at times, but in NASCAR's case, it's far less than years past.

Most Overrated Comeback Attempt
JAMES HYLTON AT THE 2007 DAYTONA 500

No 72-year-old human being should attempt to race in the Daytona 500. Nothing against the geriatric set, but a restrictor-plate race with cars inches apart at 190 mph is no place for the Medicare-eligible.

James Hylton didn't see it that way when he decided to make a comeback of sorts and attempt to qualify for the 2007 Daytona 500. His last Cup race was 14 years earlier at age 58 when he finished 34th at Darlington. Eight other times that season, he wasn't fast enough to make the starting grid. Now he planned to jump back in and race in one of NASCAR's most dangerous events at age 72, and NASCAR was going to let him do it.

"You can get yourself in trouble real quick here," Hylton said. "I'm 72, and I know I'm 72. I'm not trying to kid myself. But this isn't a publicity stunt. If anyone thinks that, they can get in the car with me when the green flag drops."

No thanks. Hylton quickly became national news. Even the late-night talk shows mentioned him. "Jay Leno got on me pretty good," Hylton said. "He said when I pit, it will be the first time a pit crew had to change a catheter. That's pretty funny."

Hylton said his car, a Chevy from Richard Childress Racing, was the best he ever had in his career. The attention for his quest even brought a sponsor on board: Retirement Living TV. "I don't think my age matters," Hylton said. "Here it's all about having people to draft with you. Carl Edwards drafted with me in testing, so he's either crazy or a really nice guy."

Senior citizens across the country e-mailed Hylton and wished him good luck. Hylton said he didn't quite have the procedure down for today's computer/Internet world. "My e-mail machine is about burned up," he said. "All us seniors aren't up on all that."

So handling e-mail on a laptop was tough, but Hylton felt up to the challenge of NASCAR's biggest event. Hylton didn't get there. He would have become the oldest driver to compete in a Nextel Cup event. Thankfully, that didn't happen. But he did compete in his Thursday qualifying race, finishing 23rd of 31 drivers. Not bad, but that was just 60 laps. The Daytona 500 is 200 laps with every driver going all out to get to the front, dependent on each other for their safety. It's no place for a septuagenarian.

CHAPTER 7

Records

The old saying that records are made to be broken doesn't always apply in NASCAR. Richard Petty's 200 career victories is one of he most unreachable records in sports—but more on that later.

Racing doesn't lend itself to a wide array of statistical records the way baseball does. For half a century, the only records anyone cared about were who won the race, who won the pole, and how many times he did it.

NASCAR officials introduced detailed statistical information three years ago known as loop data. It includes things like green flag passes, laps run in the top 15, average running position, fastest drivers on restarts, passes in the top 15, etc. The new system even has a driver rating number, similar to what the NFL does with a quarterback rating.

None of these statistics were kept in the past because the necessary technology wasn't available. The problem now is this information rarely gets used. It's still too new and too detailed for most people who cover the sport.

Many reporters find this info a little quirky and ridiculously overblown. Sort of like the baseball stat for what a hitter does against a lefthanded a pitcher in a day game with a runner in scoring position and two outs in the ninth inning. It is tedious, and only the most ardent fan (or nerd) wants to know.

For now, the loop data is too new and too unusual for most people to take it seriously and use it regularly. That will change over time as the old guard moves out and younger people (who grew up playing every high-tech video game imaginable) come in and see the information as a valuable way to evaluate driver skills.

Had all this info been available from NASCAR's inception, it would be much easier to say which records had the most meaning. No one knows exactly how many passes David Pearson made while running in the top 15. Plenty, I can assure you. When evaluating records through NASCAR's history, we'll still have to use the old-fashioned powers of observation.

Most Overrated NASCAR record
RICHARD PETTY'S 200 VICTORIES

If NASCAR races another 500 years, no one will surpass this mark. No one will come close.

It isn't that no driver has the skill to win as often as Petty did. It just can't be done anymore. In today's NASCAR, a 200-victory mark is unachievable. Petty's record is a remarkable accomplishment for any era, but it's virtually meaningless in today's version of Cup racing.

For the first 14 years of Petty career, starting in 1958, NASCAR's top series ran at least 44 races per season. That's eight more than Cup has now. Seven of those seasons had at least 50 events, and the 1964 season had 62 races. Petty competed in 61 of them. Dale Earnhardt never had more than 34 events in a season for his entire career. NASCAR had 31 races or less in each of the first 22 seasons of Earnhardt's career.

The modern era began in 1972, and Petty proved he could still drive under the new system. Four of his seven championships came from 1972 to 1979 after the schedule was shortened. But only 60 of his victories came after the 1971 season.

Petty won 140 races before the modern era began. He won 139 races on short tracks, and 30 of his victories came on dirt tracks. Some of those victories were only 100 miles or 100 laps. The last NASCAR event on dirt in the top series came in 1970, so no one competing in Cup today ever raced a Cup event on dirt.

NASCAR car owner and seven-time champion Richard Petty smiles as he watches the NASCAR Sprint Cup Series Pennsylvania 500 practice in Long Pond, Pennsylvania, on Friday, August 1, 2008.
(AP Photo/Nam Y. Huh)

Nothing against racing on dirt. It's a very specialized skill. But it's not comparable to what Cup drivers do today. Petty made 155 starts on dirt tracks. He made a total of 1,184 starts. That's another record no one will match.

If a driver started his Cup career today, assuming the schedule stays at 36 events per year, he would need to race 33 years to reach Petty's mark. It's not even a remote possibility. No active driver is within 275 starts of that total, and only drivers near the end of their careers have more than 700 starts—Kyle Petty, Michael Waltrip, and Mark Martin. Jeff Gordon and Jeff Burton have more than 500 starts, but they're not even half way to Petty's total.

The bottom line is Petty had more chances to win than any driver in history. Heck, he often got several chances in the same week. Petty won two races in one week during August of the 1962 season

Petty won races on consecutive days in Spartanburg, South Carolina, and Weaverville, North Carolina, in March of the 1963 season. During his incredible 27-win season in 1967, Petty won five races in the first 17 days of September, including two victories over a three-day span and four wins in 10 days.

Twice in the 1968 season, Petty posted two victories over a three-day span. He also won five times in the last three weeks of September. Petty won four times in July 1969, including back-to-back days at Nashville and Maryville, Tennessee.

In the final two seasons before the modern era began, Petty won 39 times in 96 races (86 starts). He won on consecutive days again in August 1970 at Winston-Salem, North Carolina, and South Boston, Virginia.

Petty's final two-wins-in-two-days effort came in July 1971 in New York state at Malta and Islip. He won four races in 18 days from July 14 to August 1. Petty also won four races over a three-week span from April 8 to April 25. Compared to Cup racing today, it's like counting wins in the B Feature of a sprint car event in Peoria.

Over a 10-year span from 1962 to 1971, Petty made 453 starts. That's an average of 10 more starts per season than a driver would have today. He won 135 races in those 10 seasons, truly remarkable, but also not in any way comparable to NASCAR is the 21st century.

By the way, Petty's 200-victory mark doesn't rank him at the top of the win percentage list. He's fourth at 16.86 percent. Herb Thomas (21.15 percent), Tim Flock (20.74 percent), and David Pearson (18.07 percent) all rank ahead of Petty among drivers with at least 100 starts.

Pearson is No. 2 on the career victories list with 105. Jeff Gordon, who entered the 2008 season with 81 victories, is the only driver with an outside shot to catch Pearson in the next few years. Of the six drivers with more than 80 victories, only Gordon and Darrell Waltrip can say all of them came in the modern era.

There's nothing wrong with Petty winning most of his races before the modern era. Winning 200 times is quite a feat no matter where or when he did it. But it isn't a valid comparison to victories earned during the last 36 years.

It's impossible to say how many times Gordon or Dale Earnhardt would have won had they raced in the 1960s when so many more events were scheduled each year. And it's impossible to say how many races Petty would have won had his career started in the early 1970s. But his 200 victories is a watered-down total when you examine the facts and see how many of those wins were accomplished.

The Rest of the Top Five
2. COMPARING CHAMPIONSHIPS

The Chase playoff format is such a radical change from the past that it's no longer possible to make valid comparisons on championships won before the Chase and the system now. Championships before 2004 were based on points accumulated for an entire season. Now those totals are reset for the final 10 races, and drivers are seeded based on races won in the regular season.

A driver could have a 300-point lead after 26 races and not start the Chase on top if someone else won the most races in the regular season. In 2007, Jeff Gordon built a 317-point lead heading into the 26th race, but he started the Chase in second place, 20 points behind teammate Jimmic Johnson.

Johnson was sixth in the points standings heading to Richmond for the last race before the Chase. He won that event to give him a season-high six victories in the first 26 races. Gordon was second with four victories. Johnson went on to win his second consecutive Cup title. It was the second time in four years that the playoff format cost Gordon the crown.

In the old system, Gordon would have clinched the 2007 championship at Texas Motor Speedway in the first weekend of November, two races before the end of the season. Gordon also would have won the title in 2004, the first year of the Chase, when Kurt Busch won the championship by eight points over Jimmie Johnson and 16 points over Gordon.

Gordon would have entered the last 10 races with a 65-point lead over Johnson and a 348-point lead over Busch. Gordon would have beaten

Johnson by 57 points, and Busch wouldn't have been a championship contender.

Under the old system, Gordon would have entered the 2008 season only one championship behind Richard Petty and Dale Earnhardt, each of whom won seven titles. Gordon's quest for the seventh championship would be the talk of the sport. His career would look much different. People would view him in a more revered fashion. At age 36 and still in his prime, Gordon would have needed only one Cup championship the rest of his career to equal those two legends. A chance at an unprecedented eighth title would have been within his reach.

Instead, he will probably fall short of catching Petty and Earnhardt for career championships. To his credit, Gordon has never complained about the new system. He understands why it was implemented and believes it has had a positive impact overall. But the Chase has clearly hurt Gordon's legacy. His fans will always feel the playoff format cost Gordon two titles, and maybe more before he quits.

Statistically speaking, that's true. But no one can say for sure Gordon would have won those two titles in 2004 and 2007 if the season-total system had been in place. The other competitors would have raced differently in the final 10 events if the playoff system wasn't in place. When Gordon was building his huge points lead in 2007, the other drivers in the top 12 weren't overly concerned about it. They knew the points would be reset in September. Making up points on Gordon wasn't their goal in the summer months. It was winning races to start the Chase in a better spot.

However you look at it, the debate over it is proof that comparing championships from vastly different systems is a waste of time. A Chase championship is a completely different accomplishment than a Cup title under the cumulative system of the past. In the Chase, a driver can get hot in the final 10 races and win a title he wouldn't have had an opportunity to win in the old system. And, as in Gordon's case, a driver can lose a championship he probably would have won easily before the Chase playoff was implemented.

The new way to compare things will be how many championships a driver won in the Chase. And for a few more years, a few drivers have a chance to say they won a title under both systems. Tony Stewart was the first to do it.

So forget about trying to figure out which driver was the best based on titles won. It no longer applies.

3. CAREER EARNINGS

For his first victory in 1960 at Charlotte, Richard Petty won $800. For victory No. 200 in the Firecracker 400 at Daytona on July 4, 1984, Petty won $43,755. The lowest payout for any driver at any race in 2007 was $61,030 to Dale Jarrett for his 42nd-place finish at Pocono in August.

It's fun to look at how much these guys make in a race, but it is preposterous to compare career earnings as a way to determine just how good a driver was in his day. Petty never made a million dollars in a season. He made more than $500,000 only twice—1979 and 1983. Gordon has never had a season when he made less than $500,000. He earned $765,168 his rookie year of 1993.

As early as 1998, Gordon earned more purse money ($9,306,584) than Petty earned in his 35-year career ($8,541,210). In 2008, Gordon became the first NASCAR driver in history to reach $100 million in earnings. But let's compare start by start. At the end of the 2007 season, Gordon had averaged $183,313 in earnings for each Cup start, including end-of-the-season bonus money. Petty's average purse per start was $7,214.

Jimmie Johnson earned $31.2 million for his back-to-back championship seasons of 2006 and 2007. In his first six Cup seasons, Johnson earned $59.5 million. At that rate, Johnson would reach $100 million in just a little more than 10 seasons.

That pretty much tells you all you need to know. But the problem with an earnings ranking goes deeper than the dramatic differences in compensation over the years. No purse payoff system in all of professional sports is as ridiculously convoluted as earnings in a NASCAR race. One would assume that a driver who finishes 15th would earn more money than a driver who finishes 20th, but it doesn't always work that way with a NASCAR purse.

As an example, let's look at the 2008 Daytona 500. Brian Vickers finished 12th and made $285,245. Jeff Gordon finished 39th and made $319,599. Fourteen drivers who finished below Vickers earned more money for their effort. Gordon made more money than 21 drivers who finished ahead of him.

How about a system where a driver makes more than the other guy by outracing him? Apparently, that's too much to ask. This formula is confusing and infuriating for many fans. I receive dozens of emails every year from people seeking an explanation of the NASCAR payout on races. They don't get it, and they aren't alone. I don't get it, either. Even some drivers and crew chiefs don't get it, but I'll try to explain it as best I can.

Where a driver finishes is only part of the purse money awarded at each race. The payout includes a lot for extra awards that fans don't understand—qualifying bonuses, television money, manufacturer awards, sponsor award programs, and a prorated portion of the points fund.

TV money and the basic purse are distributed as one would expect—the winner gets the most and the last-place finisher the least. After that, things get complicated.

Teams get a certain amount of money at each event based on which manufacturer decals they have on the car. That's why cars have all those little decals behind the front tire. It all depends on which sponsors your team has and what the agreement is.

NASCAR also has several special plans that add purse money to the top drivers and teams. One plan is the Winner's Circle program, which pays a bonus to the top 10 winners from the previous season and the first two new winners of an ongoing season. Teams that ranked in the top 30 from the previous season also receive a purse bonus.

In other words, it's a jigsaw puzzle of money and awards that's impossible for fans to decipher. But it's also another reason why career earnings are meaningless for judging performance. Where a driver finishes doesn't equate to what he's paid, so what he earns doesn't tell you much, except that all these guys are getting rich.

4. RICHARD PETTY'S 126 POLES

This isn't as much of a knock on Petty's mark as it is a criticism of pole records in general. At least in Petty's day, winning the pole was often a good indication that a driver had the best car and should be considered a favorite to win. Winning a pole these days rarely means a race victory, unless it happens on a road course.

In 2007, the pole sitter won only four of 36 Cup races. The Happy Hour final practice session is often a better indicator of how a driver will perform in the race. With some impound races, teams with guaranteed spots in the field don't make a serious effort to win the pole. So pole records aren't so hot.

In Petty's case, poles had a little more meaning, but the man had 1,184 starts to get his 126 poles. David Pearson won 112 poles in only 574 starts. Petty's pole percentage is 10.6 percent. Pearson's is 19.5 percent. But in general, who cares? Where you start isn't the goal. It's where you finish.

5. RICHARD PETTY'S 13 CONSECUTIVE YEARS WITH A WIN FROM THE POLE

This is one of 13 driver records NASCAR lists in the annual Cup Media Guide. Isn't this something a driver would be expected to do? If you start first on a regular basis, logic tells us you should win some of those events.

Besides, this is a little like making a big deal out of the number of consecutive years Brett Favre threw a touchdown pass, or the number of consecutive years Babe Ruth hit a home run. If they were competing, they were doing it. Well, not entirely. Petty won races in 18 consecutive years, so for five of those seasons, he didn't win a race from the pole.

Most Underrated Record
RICKY RUDD'S 788 CONSECUTIVE STARTS

This is the Iron Man record for all of sports. Yeah, I know. Cal Ripken Jr. passed the great Lou Gehrig in the cherished Major League Baseball record for consecutive games played. Ripken played in an amazing 2,632 consecutive baseball games over 16 seasons.

Driver Ricky Rudd, left, receives an "Iron Man" award from Terry Labonte, right, during a news conference at Lowe's Motor Speedway in Concord, North Carolina, on Thursday, May 16, 2002. (AP Photo/Chuck Burton)

However, I don't think Ripken ever had to tape his eyelids open so he could field ground balls or hit a hanging curve. Rudd made that unusual adjustment so he could see to drive a race car at 200 mph for three hours, keeping the streak alive.

Rudd raced hurt more times than he can remember, staying in the driver's seat and racing week after week for 25 seasons. His streak began at Riverside, California, on January 11, 1981, and continued until the end of the 2005 season.

"I think it says a little bit about your character," Rudd once said in a teleconference about his streak. "There were plenty of days I'd much rather have been lying in a hospital bed than sitting in the race car."

Rudd should have watched from a hospital bed several times. The streak would have ended after three years. Rudd suffered numerous injuries in

1984 when his car became a bowling pin, flipping over several times in a violent crash during the Shootout All-Star race at Daytona the week before the Daytona 500. Rudd suffered torn cartilage in his ribcage. The man had to strain just to breathe. He also had a concussion and bruises covered his face—both of his eyes were swollen shut. Rocky Balboa looked better after his first fight with Apollo Creed.

"I took a trip to the hospital and, really, they wanted to keep me there quite a bit longer than I wanted to stay," Rudd said. "I basically checked myself out the next morning."

But Rudd needed to come up with an unusual medical treatment device if he was going to drive in the Daytona 500. Rudd taped his eyelids open with duct tape so he could see. He finished seventh. "It probably wasn't real smart of me to be driving," he said. "I basically focused on the back bumper of the car in front of me. It was about all I could see."

Rudd was still hurting a week later, but he won the following weekend at Richmond. "That was pretty emotional," Rudd said. "The wreck [at Daytona] was close to being a career-ending situation, so to win the race at Richmond after that was a great feeling."

Another example of Rudd racing hurt came after his car slammed into the wall at Charlotte in 1988, tearing the ligaments in his left knee. Doctors told Rudd he needed immediate surgery, which would have kept him out of the car for at least six weeks. Rudd said no way. He flew to Indianapolis and saw an orthopedic specialist who designed a special knee brace that Rudd could use in the car.

Rudd finished seventh at North Wilkesboro, North Carolina, the week after the accident. "The only trouble was I couldn't use my left leg at all, so they had the team work and put in a hand clutch for pit stops," Rudd said. "Once I got off pit road, I could hand shift it and not use a clutch."

Rudd did whatever it took to keep racing. Among active drivers, no one is close to equaling his mark. At the end of the 2007 season, Jeff Gordon had made 509 consecutive starts. That is a record of its own as the most consecutive starts from the beginning of a driver's Cup career. However, catching Rudd isn't likely. Gordon would need to race in every event into the middle of the 2015 season to surpass Rudd's mark. Gordon would be 44 years old.

In past eras, that's no big deal age-wise, but Gordon has said repeatedly that he doesn't plan to do this in his mid-40s. The man is wealthy. *Forbes* magazine estimated his 2007 income at $32 million. Gordon is also a national celebrity outside of racing. He's part of the jet set, spending his off season in a penthouse apartment in Manhattan. Gordon has a lot of interests, so unless he's chasing that seventh title at 44, he will probably move on with his life.

That's also true of most future drivers who might have a shot at Rudd's mark. In one respect, it's easier to do now because there's far less chance that a driver would suffer an injury that would keep him out of the car. But the money thing gets in the way. Cup drivers make so much money now that it isn't necessary to keep racing into their late 40s. Cup also has the longest season in major professional sports, starting in early February and ending in late November. It's a grind that doesn't sound too appealing at 45.

Gordon might get as high as third on the all-time list, passing former teammate Terry Labonte's consecutive starts total of 655 races, but Rusty Wallace looks secure in the No. 2 spot with 697 consecutive starts.

Rudd did a few other impressive things in his career, including at least one victory in 16 consecutive seasons. He started racing in Cup at 18 years old and competed for the last time at Homestead-Miami Speedway in the final event of the 2007 season at age 51. He is the only man to win the Brickyard 400 at Indianapolis as a driver/owner of a single-car team, accomplishing the feat in 1997 at age 40. Don't look for that to happen again.

Rudd won't go down as one of the best drivers in NASCAR history. But he may always hold a record that shows dedication, desire, sacrifice, and personal strength of character. Rudd's record of 788 consecutive starts shines brightly in racing and compares favorably to all of the Iron Man marks in athletics.

The Rest of the Top Five
2. DALE INMAN'S EIGHT CHAMPIONSHIPS AS A CREW CHIEF

No one in NASCAR history has done what Dale Inman did. Not Richard Petty. Not Dale Earnhardt. Inman's eight championships as a crew chief stand alone when you start listing titles in NASCAR's top series.

Seven of those championships came with Richard Petty, who is Inman's cousin. Some people believe Petty would have won those titles no matter who was on the pit box. It isn't true, but Inman proved he could win with someone else when he got championship No. 8. The 1984 Cup championship he earned with Terry Labonte is probably Inman's shining moment. It was Labonte's first Cup title after finishing fifth in the standings in 1983. Labonte only won twice in 1984, but he posted top-10 finishes in 24 of 30 races, including 17 top-5 finishes.

Labonte was younger and less experienced than most of the other drivers in the top 10, but he had the most experienced crew chief in Inman. Inman later returned to Petty Enterprises and was there when Richard retired in 1992. Inman continued to work in NASCAR through the 1998 season before retiring from the sport.

Inman's biggest asset was a skill that all crew chiefs need—an instinctive ability to make the right call at the crucial moment of a race. Maybe the best example of it was the 1981 Daytona 500 when Petty won the event for the seventh and final time. Petty trailed Bobby Allison by six seconds, but Inman took a chance at the end. Instead of changing tires, Inman opted to go with fuel only in Petty's final stop with 24 laps remaining. It put Petty in front, and the old tires were good enough to hold off Allison at the end.

Kirk Shelmerdine is the only other crew chief with more than three championships, guiding Dale Earnhardt to four of his titles. But Inman is also the only crew chief with five championships in the modern area.

Inman led his drivers to 193 victories, the only crew chief with more than 100 victories. He was only 28 when he led Petty to his first championship in 1964.

3. ALAN KULWICKI'S 1992 COMEBACK TO WIN THE CHAMPIONSHIP

Officially, this isn't even a record. Darrell Waltrip overcame a 341-point deficit to win the Cup title in 1981. But Waltrip had 17 races to make up the ground and get to the top, winning the crown by 53 points over Bobby Allison. Only half of the season was complete when Waltrip found himself 341 points down.

Kulwicki had a far more difficult task. He made up 278 points in only six races. He edged Bill Elliott by 10 points at the end, making up an average of 48 points in each race for the last six weeks of the season. Kulwicki won the pole at Dover on September 20 but counted himself out after he crashed in the race and finished 34th.

"This probably finishes us off in the championship deal," a dejected Kulwicki said that day at Dover.

But Kulwicki was only 30 points behind Davey Allison going into the final race at Atlanta. Elliott was 40 points behind Allison. Kulwicki was the clear underdog against rising star Allison and former champ Elliott. Kulwicki enjoyed the role, even getting Ford and NASCAR officials to allow him to change the lettering on the front of his car from Thunderbird to Underbird. Elliott won the race, but Kulwicki's second-place showing was good enough to claim the season title.

Kulwicki was killed in a place crash less than five months later, but his remarkable comeback will always stand out as one of the top achievements in NASCAR history.

4. DALE EARNHARDT'S 174 CONSECUTIVE RACES RANKED IN THE TOP 10

Earnhardt did many remarkable things in his legendary career, but maintaining his ranking in the top 10 for every race over the course of seven seasons has to be among the most impressive accomplishments in racing.

From February 23, 1986, until March 1, 1992, Earnhardt never dropped out of the top 10. He earned four of his seven Cup championships and won 37 races during that span. He finished second and third in the two seasons he didn't win the title during that streak.

To really appreciate the achievement, you have to realize how easy it would have been to fall below the top 10. All it would have taken was a bad finish in one of the first two or three events of each season. To stay in the top 10 that long meant Earnhardt had to finish in the top 10 in the season-opening Daytona 500 for six consecutive seasons. Earnhardt had four top-5 finishes, one ninth, and one 10th-place finish in the 500 during the streak.

Earnhardt also had two other streaks of more than 100 races where he stayed in the top 10.

5. JEFF GORDON'S 10 CONSECUTIVE SEASONS OF 20 OR MORE TOP-10 FINISHES

Gordon finished in the top 10 in 230 of 339 races from 1995 through 2004, an incredible 68 percent of the events on the Cup schedule. And he managed to post at least 20 top-10 finishes in each of those seasons.

No one else has equaled the 20-in-10 mark. Lee Petty fell one top 10 short of that mark in the 1950 season. Petty had nine consecutive seasons with at least 20 top-10 finishes from 1952-60. He had 19 top-10 finishes in 1951. But Petty competed in 395 events over than span, 56 more than Gordon had in his 10 years to set the record.

Richard Petty had a record 18 seasons of 10 or more top-10 finishes, but he didn't string 10 in a row as Gordon did. Petty's longest streak was seven years (1966-72). Goodness knows he had a lot more opportunities. Six times in his career, The King posted more top-10 finishes in a season than the number of events Gordon has ever raced in one year. Petty's longest streak in the modern era was only four years (1974-77).

Mark Martin had seven consecutive years with at least 20 top-10 finishes from 1994-2000 in the No. 6 Ford for Roush Racing. But Gordon's mark is the one the younger guys will have to shoot for to achieve an unmatched level of excellence.

CHAPTER 8

Events

The Cup Series races at 23 speedways over a 10-month schedule. Fourteen tracks play host to two Cup events a year. Eight others have only one Cup race each season. A few tracks that have two events should only have one (or none). A few speedways that have only one race should have two. And at least one track that doesn't have a Cup race (Kentucky) has proven it deserves one.

The Cup schedule is always a work in progress that's subject to change from year to year. Officially, every sanctioning agreement between NASCAR and a speedway is negotiated on a one-year basis.

Unofficially, there are some sacred cows out there that won't lose their Cup date unless the place burns down. International Speedway Corporation, which owns 12 facilities that play host to 19 Cup events each year, is a sister company to NASCAR. The France family owns NASCAR and has controlling interest in ISC. Consequently, an ISC track isn't losing a Cup date unless it goes to a new ISC facility or someone pays a huge amount of money for it.

Not matter who owns it, having a Cup event is a little like being a tenured professor. You have to do something really bad to lose your position. Most events accomplish the main goals—make lots of money by putting on a reasonably good show in a comfortable atmosphere.

Some are better at it than others, of course. So let's look at some NASCAR events that stand out, or don't stand out, as the case may be.

All-Star Races
1. MOST UNDERRATED ALL-STAR RACE: THE BUDWEISER SHOOTOUT

This is equivalent to a one-game preseason involving some of the biggest stars of the sport, and they actually care about winning. The NFL should take note: One-and-done before the real season begins for each team. Winning teams get a bonus check to split; losers get nothing. Now there's a preseason weekend I'd watch.

NASCAR Winston Cup Series drivers start the Budweiser Shootout on Saturday night, February 8, 2003, at Daytona International Speedway in Daytona Beach, Florida. The Shootout was run under the lights for the first time. (AP Photo/Terry Renna)

The NFL bores us to tears each summer with more than a month of pre-season games featuring players who won't be in the league come mid-September. Major League Baseball teams play 30 or so spring games that most players consider a glorified fitness program.

A major league team's ace tossing three innings in a Class A park and hitting the showers before hitting golf balls that afternoon doesn't tell me much. But watching rookie Denny Hamlin bump-draft with the best and win the 2007 Bud Shootout—his first Cup race at Daytona—told me a lot. "That was a great boost to our team," said Hamlin, who went on to make the Chase and finish third in the standings. "Winning the Bud Shootout will mean a lot to me the rest of my career."

That's the point. It means something. No one is going through the motions at the expense of the ticket buyers. No starting quarterback is playing two series then taking a powder.

"Points don't matter, and second place means nothing," said Mark Martin. "You have everyone out there really going for it all and trying to get the win."

This is NASCAR's one-and-only preseason event. More than $1 million is on the line. The sport's biggest stars are going all out at NASCAR's top venue. Now that's an exhibition season fans can appreciate. The 70-lap show isn't a test run to see who can make your race team. It's about flooring it in an all-out sprint.

The Bud Shootout at Daytona doesn't count toward who wins the championship, but it does start the season with a meaningful show where the competitors are racing hard for a victory. In fact, it's more about winning than the 36 points-paying races. With no points on the line and no position in the standings to protect, it's a rare chance to go for broke. Drivers can get racy, show what they've got, and make their sponsors proud.

NASCAR changed the qualifications rules for 2009 to allow equal representation for each auto manufacturer. The 24 drivers eligible to compete are the top six by manufacturer—Chevrolet, Ford, Dodge, and Toyota—in the previous season's standings. This is one thing NASCAR gets right.

The race is usually a sheet-metal bashing event that gives the fans a heck of a show. It's one race, for one night, one week before NASCAR's season-opening event. It's not four or five meaningless NFL football games with players who won't be around once the real season starts. No month-long boredom on the diamonds of Florida and Arizona with guys playing half-speed in facilities they won't see when the actual seasons starts, as MLB does.

The Saturday night Bud Shootout is real racing and serious competition for the drivers involved, including more than $1 million on the line for the participants. The race is two segments: 25 laps of feeling things out, a 10-minute break, and then 50 laps to the finish that often include some wild moments down the stretch.

It also gives the drivers valuable track time one week before the most important event of the season—the Daytona 500. Drivers don't use the car they will drive in the 500. Usually it's the back-up car. Knowing how wild things get in the Shootout, it wouldn't make sense to risk wrecking your best car.

"It's just a no-holds-barred great race for the fans and the drivers," Jimmie Johnson said. "And it's a great way to get back in the groove without the added pressure of knowing points are on the line."

Past Shootout results were often a good predictor of things to come. Five times, the Shootout winner has taken the checkered flag in the big race one week later. Jarrett has three Shootout wins. Two of those years (1996 and 2000), he went on to win the Daytona 500.

Since its inception in 1979, the Shootout winner became that season's Cup champion seven times. Sounds significant to me.

It's preseason the way it ought to be. Call it immediate gratification. For any fan with a short attention span, it's the perfect way to start.

Most Overrated All-Star Race
THE SPRINT CUP CHALLENGE

The annual Nextel All-Star Challenge has produced some exciting racing over the years, but calling it an All-Star event is a bit of a stretch. The 2007 race automatically included Casey Mears and Brain Vickers, two guys who hadn't reached All-Star quality. It also included Dale Jarrett and Bobby

Labonte, former Cup champs who weren't having anything close to an All-Star season. Speaking of non–All-Stars, Michael Waltrip actually won this thing once.

On the other end of things was Carl Edwards. He ranked 10th in the standings going into the All-Star race weekend, but he didn't have a guaranteed spot. Failing to guarantee a spot for Edwards and Clint Bowyer—two guys who made the Chase in 2007 and ranked among the leaders in the standings that May—also missed the All-Star concept.

Making an adjustment to rectify that flaw would require another format change to an event that changes more than the NASCAR rulebook. Here's a test. In a minute or less, tell me the entire All-Star race format and qualifying rules. If you were able to do that in 60 seconds or less, see a psychiatrist immediately. You really need to get out more.

A new plan was revealed in January 2007. It was listed on a poster board that resembled an MIT professor's equation for nuclear fusion. The main show consists of four 20-lap segments (or quarters) with no caution laps counted in the last segment.

Drivers get in based on a long list of criteria: Winners from the previous season and the current season (drivers or car if the driver changed teams), past Cup champions, and previous All-Star winners from the past 10 years. Then there's the qualifying race. The top two finishers from the open qualifier (40 laps over two 20-lap segments) also make it. One lucky driver gets voted in by the fans, but he has to finish on the lead lap in the Open. Excuse me while I go take a couple of Tylenol (the official pain reliever of NASCAR) to ease the throbbing pain in my head from explaining all that mess.

It's easy to see why the casual fan doesn't really understand how this thing works. But once you get past the constantly shifting and convoluted rules, the on-track action is usually a heck of a show. No points are on the line, so drivers can go all out and get wild to try to earn that $1 million victory prize. The event has given fans some memorable moments.

The only problem is they've all come at Lowe's Motor Speedway, except for the 1986 event at Atlanta Motor Speedway. Nothing against the folks at Lowe's—they rank among the best at promoting an event—but true All-Star shows should move around. Otherwise you become the NFL Pro Bowl in Hawaii, the most meaningless All-Star game in sports.

The drivers and crews don't want the All-Star race to leave Charlotte, where the NASCAR teams are based. It gives everyone an extra week at home and a break from the brutal travel schedule (38 events in 41 weeks) of the Cup season. But the schedule includes seven points races (two at Lowe's, two at Bristol, two at Martinsville, and one at Darlington) that are less than a two-hour drive away.

An All-Star event is primarily for the fans. Instead of constantly changing the format to keep things fresh at the same venue, keep the format the same and change the venue. Speedway Motorsports Inc. mogul Bruton Smith continues to lobby for a second Cup date at Las Vegas Motor Speedway, so why not move the All-Star race to Vegas? Lowe's and Las Vegas fall under the SMI umbrella. Smith could easily make the move with a little coaxing. The entire atmosphere around the All-Star event is a glitzy, super-hyped show, which is a perfect fit for Las Vegas.

Another thought is to move the event from year to year among several worthy locations. Imagine how crazy things would get with an All-Star race on the half-mile oval at Bristol. Maybe the All-Star event is just what Auto Club Speedway in California needs to garner more interest from the Hollywood crowd.

Give the sparkling Kansas City track (another facility with only one Cup event) host duties one year. Holding the event at nontraditional NASCAR markets is a great way to increase the fan base. Moving the event to other parts of the country would generate buzz about how the race would play out on a different track.

NASCAR could also consider rotating the event to tracks that don't have a Cup date—Nashville, Iowa, Milwaukee, or Kentucky.

Having the race at Lowe's every year is a little like playing every Major League Baseball All-Star game at Yankee Stadium. You need some venue diversity to keep it interesting. Making this event the best it can be isn't difficult—move it around, simplify the format, and make sure the best drivers are in the race.

Most Overrated Event
THE SPRINT CUP AWARDS BANQUET

Almost everyone involved in the Cup Series enjoys going to New York City in early December for the Champions Week in the Big Apple. It's play time in Manhattan for the teams that enjoyed some success that season.

This is the opposite end of the spectrum from Talladega. National TV show appearances, a victory lap in Times Square, lunch and dinner at five-star restaurants, cocktail parties with the corporate suits, dancing at hip-and-trendy nightclubs...it's all part of the fun.

The week of celebration leads up to the nationally televised Cup Awards Ceremony on Friday night at the Waldorf-Astoria. All that excitement, then a three-hour snoozer. As I wrote in 2007, it's a season filled with dramatic moments that ends with a black-tie show totally devoid of drama. It's not part of the plan.

Yes, the drivers and their significant others all look delightful in formal attire. While it's great to honor the top 10 and see them give a (hopefully) short speech on stage, exciting it ain't. The event has the thrill factor of a parade lap at Pocono.

This is the only major awards show where all the winners are known before the ceremony begins. Would you watch the Daytona 500 if you knew who the winner was before the green flag dropped? (Well, maybe all you Dale Earnhardt Jr. fans would do it if psychic John Edward phoned before the race to tell you he saw Junior win.)

The point is NASCAR's postseason awards show needs some sizzle. NASCAR officials have tried to add some spice in recent years with celebrity involvement. Comedian Jay Mohr hosted the show for three years. He always added some funny moments—including a few that required a bleep or two. David Spade added a few chuckles to the 2007 show, as well.

NASCAR has even thrown in some decent singers the last couple of years, including Jewel and Kelly Clarkson. NASCAR also added a nice segment in 2007 showing video with the drivers and their families, a personal touch that portrayed a side of the drivers the fans rarely see.

It's worth tuning in, but this show is a little like watching a 400-lap race without a single pass for the lead. Interesting, but it isn't edge-of-your-seat entertainment. Some of it is unavoidable. Obviously, we know going in who finished where in the Cup standings. So adding some unknowns to the night wouldn't hurt. Sprint and NASCAR took a step in the right direction in 2006 with the fan vote for the Most Dramatic Moment of the season. Fans have five options, and the winner is announced during the telecast.

It isn't enough.

Why not add some awards and have the nominees in the audience? Make the event similar to other awards shows. Teams could vote on an annual Sportsmanship Award, Comeback Driver of the Year, Crew Chief of the Year, etc. Pick five nominees in each category and open the envelope that night—now you have something to watch.

People watch racing because you never know what might happen. So why have an awards night with that element missing? Make it fun. How about an award for the Best Paint Scheme? Or Best NASCAR Commercial of the Year? Sponsors would love those two, and we know NASCAR is all about the sponsors.

Thanking sponsors is one of the problems on awards night. Every driver has to mention every sponsor of his team. It's understandable. Any company willing to spend $15 to $20 million a year to sponsor a car deserves some recognition. But it's sooooo boring. Why not run a crawl at the bottom of the screen listing the sponsors of the driver speaking at the podium?

Most drivers are pros at speaking to reporters, but talking in front of a huge audience is entirely different. "They all were going long on their speeches," NASCAR's senior communications manager Herb Branham told me in 2007. "So we opted to start helping some of them a few years ago. But we don't edit what they want to say. We just help them say it more succinctly."

Branham does a superb job of scripting what the drivers tell him. Unfortunately, some of them just read the prompter in a monotone. They seem like mannequins with robotic mouths. The best ones are guys who ad-lib a little and go off script. Tony Stewart has it down pat. He got in a quick joke on NASCAR vice president Jim Hunter and NASCAR president Mike Helton to start his championship speech in 2006. "I'll try to hurry this along," Stewart said. "I notice that Jim Hunter is running out of wine over there, so I know he's anxious to get out of here. And I'm sure Helton's right behind him."

Of course, by that time, many viewers already had gone night-night from the earlier speeches. All awards shows have moments that cure insomnia. Does anyone really care who wins for Best Sound Editing at the Academy Awards? Maybe not, but at least you know there's a payoff if you manage to stay awake until the end.

It's like watching a race. You sit through a bunch of uneventful laps to see who wins at the finish. We all know who wins while watching the Cup Awards, but at least give us a few moments of suspense along the way.

Most Overrated Decision on Cup Events
LATE AFTERNOON START TIMES

For many years, NASCAR fans were accustomed to watching Cup races that started around lunch time on the East Coast. Fans in other parts of the country knew the Sunday NASCAR race took place early in the day. But NASCAR officials decided a few years ago that later was better. The thought was that starting races later in the afternoon would bring higher television ratings.

Speedway officials also liked the idea because fans had more time to spend money at the track before the race began. It also led to some day-night races at tracks with lights. The events start in daylight and end at night. This allowed some races to finish in prime time for television viewers.

But the later starts have not generated the increased viewer interest that NASCAR envisioned. In 2008, NASCAR officials said some races would return to start times earlier in the day, but most stayed the same. The Daytona 500, which for years started at 12:30 PM EST, began at 3:30 PM.

This trend started years ago in other sports. Every World Series game and every NBA Finals game start at night, often ending after midnight in the Eastern time zone. The Super Bowl begins at 6:00 PM EST.

NASCAR fans were accustomed to starting their Sunday afternoons with a green flag and seeing the race end by mid-afternoon. Some of those fans have since found other things to do instead of waiting for a race to start later in the day.

Other Overrated Events
RACES WITH A 500-MILE DISTANCE

Even 100 miles less than the Coca-Cola 600 is still too much at most events. With the exception of the Daytona 500 and maybe one of the Talladega races, no Cup event needs to go 500 miles. That distance isn't necessary to determine which driver has the best car and best crew on that particular day. A distance of 400 miles is plenty to decide the outcome in a fair way.

Many of the 500-mile events take too long to complete. Surpassing three hours is more than an average person's attention span can handle. The two Pocono races are the best examples of races that never seem to end. This list should also include some races at short tracks that are 500 laps. The 2007 fall race on the half-mile oval at Martinsville took four hours to complete. The spring race was 3 hours, 44 minutes.

The 500-mile race at Darlington and the 500-miler at Lowe's were also four hours. NASCAR had 14 Cup races in 2007 that were 3 hours, 28 minutes or longer. By comparison, the Boston Red Sox were playing the longest games in the first half of the 2008 season. STATS LLC listed the average length of a Red Sox game at 3 hours, 6 minutes. Major League Baseball, the NFL, and college football have all taken steps to shorten the length of games in recent years. NASCAR should follow suit.

Other motor sports leagues already have much shorter races than Sprint Cup. The longest Formula One race in 2007 was the European Grand Prix in Valencia, Spain. It took only 2 hours, 6 minutes to complete. The longest distance for an F1 event is 310 kilometers (about 192 miles) for the Valencia event at the Malaysian Grand Prix.

Shorter races sure haven't hurt F1's popularity. In fact, I would argue that it helps because fans don't have to devote half of their Sunday to watching the event. The Indy 500 is the only 500-mile event in the IndyCar Series and the only race on the schedule that takes more than three hours to complete.

NASCAR keeps droning along with races that have laps seemingly into infinity. Two big problems stand in the way of reducing the length of races. First, as far as track owners are concerned, the longer the better. More time at the track equals more beer, hot dogs, cotton candy, etc. sold to paying customers. Second, longer telecasts also mean more time for the television networks to sell the advertising that pays the enormous price required to secure the broadcast rights for these events.

There has to be a middle ground for compromise to make some of these races shorter, tightening the drama and keeping the viewers entertained from start to finish.

One other thing—at a time when gas prices are soaring and forcing paying customers to cut back on their travel plans, shouldn't NASCAR send a message that it is also cutting back on its fuel usage?

COCA-COLA 600

If a typical 500-mile race is too long, 100 more miles doesn't make it better. The ultimate endurance race in NASCAR had its place at one time, but now it's an unnecessary marathon. Skip the middle 300 laps and come back for the last 50 to see the real excitement.

Almost five hours of racing 400 grueling laps is more time than the average fan wants to invest in watching a race. The event is about staying out of trouble for 350 laps and hoping you're still in position to win it in the last 50. Not many drivers have a chance at the end because most of them aren't on the lead lap.

Unless NASCAR plans a 24-hour event to really test a team's endurance, 600 miles doesn't yield anything more than we learn from teams in 500 or 400 miles, except accumulating more laps where nothing much happens.

Most Underrated Event for Change
THE ALLSTATE 400 AT THE BRICKYARD

Yes, yes. In the speedways chapter, I listed Indianapolis Motor Speedway as No. 2 on the most overrated list. That's true for the actual racing on the giant rectangle, along with some of the problems with the amenities at the old facility.

But as I pointed out earlier, this event had historic implications for NASCAR's growth. For decades, even the suggestion of a NASCAR race at

The field heads into the first turn on the start of the NASCAR Allstate 400 at the Brickyard at the Indianapolis Motor Speedway, on Sunday, August 7, 2005, in Indianapolis.
(AP Photo/John Harrell)

Indy was more than absurd. It was sacrilege. A car with fenders racing at Indy? Ridiculous!

When the day finally came 15 years ago, auto racing in America was transformed forever. NASCAR came of age in 1994 when an up-and-coming kid named Jeff Gordon, who spent his teenage years a few miles from the storied speedway, won the inaugural Brickyard 400. It also didn't hurt when NASCAR's biggest star—Dale Earnhardt—won at Indy one year later.

The controversial decision to bring NASCAR to Indy was an overwhelming success. The doubters were silenced, and there were plenty of doubters. Many open-wheel devotees were angry when IMS owner Tony George cut a deal with NASCAR chairman Bill France Jr. and agreed to bring a NASCAR race to the hallowed grounds.

At the time, people wondered whether big stock cars would fit on the narrow Indy asphalt. Could they get through the four turns without a demolition derby on every lap? And it was up for debate whether local racing fans would show up. Some folks thought the endeavor was destined to fail. Oh, how wrong they were.

The debut event had more people in the grandstands (more than 250,000) than any stock car race in history. Clearly, it was meant to be. NASCAR's popularity was growing rapidly in the mid-1990s, but success at Indianapolis brought a new form of legitimacy to a sport often seen in the past as a Southern phenomenon.

Competing at the shrine of auto racing was a big step toward moving NASCAR from a regional sport into the national mainstream. NASCAR wasn't just for the good old boys drinking sweet tea and eating corn bread. It was a sport for everyone in all parts of the country.

Racing on the 2.5-mile rectangle was the catalyst for change. Saying you were a NASCAR fan became a cool thing. Maybe it wasn't hip and trendy, but NASCAR was heading that way. A giant crowd at Indianapolis proved NASCAR was bigger than many people imagined.

The boom was underway. NASCAR officials knew that expansion and realignment to new locales would work. Within five years of the first race at Indy, NASCAR was racing at new facilities in major markets, including

Los Angeles, Dallas/Fort Worth, Miami, and Las Vegas. In 2001, two other new facilities (Kansas Speedway and Chicagoland Speedway in Joliet, Illinois) made Kansas City and Chicago part of the NASCAR nation.

While NASCAR was growing, open-wheel racing was destroying itself. Two years after NASCAR came to Indy, American open-wheel racing underwent a nasty, name-calling split into two separate leagues. The glory days of the Indy 500 were over. It hasn't been the same since.

The two open-wheel leagues (the IRL and Champ Car) finally merged at the start of 2008, but it will take years, if ever, for Indy-car racing to return to its past glory. Indianapolis residents and die-hard open-wheel fans hate to hear it, but during the split, the Allstate 400 at the Brickyard was the biggest event at IMS each year. More people showed up for Cup qualifying than for Pole Day of the Indy 500.

The Allstate 400 is considered by most NASCAR racers to be the second biggest event in the sport after the Daytona 500. It certainly pays that way, providing the second highest purse in Cup. Fans may argue over which events rate as NASCAR's majors, but everyone agrees this race is one of them.

There's only one problem: The on-track racing at Indy won't rank among the most exciting tracks for Cup events. Side-by-side action with lots of passing just doesn't happen here with stock cars. Fans don't seem to care. They come to see the stars of the sport, and the stars have shined at Indy. Gordon joined the Indy legends when he won his fourth Allstate 400 in 2004. A fifth Indy victory would tie him with Formula One legend Michael Schumacher, who won five times on the Brickyard road course at the U.S. Grand Prix.

From 1998 through 2007, six Indy winners went on to win the Cup championship that season. That included Tony Stewart in 2005, when the Indiana boy got his lifelong wish by taking the checkered flag at the place he loves.

Dreams come true at Indianapolis, like NASCAR's dream of reaching the big time. When that first green flag waved in 1994, NASCAR found something it needed.

Indy was an important showcase for NASCAR, a platform that helped the sport transition from the backwoods to corporate boardrooms. Acceptance and respect at the Brickyard were the keys that opened those doors.

Other Underrated Events
FORD 400 AT HOMESTEAD-MIAMI SPEEDWAY

Since the track was reconfigured, the 1.5-mile oval has produced some exciting racing to end the Cup season. Consider these stats from the 2007 season: The Homestead race had 25 lead changes among 11 drivers. Las Vegas was the only event that did better on a track of the same size at the same distance with 28 lead changes among 16 drivers. If you take the equivalent percentage for the 500 or 600-mile races on 1.5-mile ovals, none of them equal Homestead for passing up front.

Homestead gets a bad rap because the place was a disaster when it was a miniature version of the Indianapolis Motor Speedway, but it's been a good place to race since the transition of the turns was changed and additional banking was added. A 400-mile event on a racy track in sunny South Florida is a nice way to end the season.

THE JUNE RACE AT MICHIGAN SPEEDWAY

Another event that has a bad reputation, but it isn't as boring as people would have you believe. The track is so wide that it produces multiple grooves and a fair share of side-by-side racing. Like most big tracks running the Car of Tomorrow, passing up front is difficult. That will improve as the teams get more accustomed to the intricacies of the new car.

The real reason some fans dislike Michigan is the fact that the 2-mile oval doesn't have a lot of wrecks. The width of the track enables drivers to avoid each other when something goes wrong. So the races have a lot of long green-flag runs. When that happens, fuel strategy often plays a part in who wins the race. Fans don't want to see races decided on fuel strategy. But the legion of Dale Earnhardt Jr. fans weren't complaining in June 2008 when he ended his 76-race losing streak by gambling on fuel at Michigan.

Those fuel strategy complaints depend on who wins and who loses, but Michigan does have some passing. In 2007, the two Michigan events had 40 lead changes among 21 drivers in a total of 400 laps. The two races at the enormously popular Bristol Motor Speedway had 26 lead changes among 18 drivers in 1,000 laps. But Bristol usually has a lot of wrecking and banging sheet metal. Michigan doesn't.

It just depends on how you look at it and what makes you happy. The Cup schedule has a lot of events with less side-by-side racing and fewer lead passes than the two at Michigan, so why didn't I list both Michigan events? Because two races at the same spot running the same distance only two months apart is another reason people view Michigan as a little boring.

Spice it up, and make the second race 300 miles. Or better yet, add lights and make the second one a Saturday night event.

CHAPTER 9

Drivers of Yesteryear, Past Generations, and One-Win Wonders

As tough as it is to rate modern-era drivers, it's even more difficult to judge the men who did this in the old days. For one thing, not as much statistical information is available to make comparisons. Another problem is the car was a much bigger factor in how well a driver performed 50 years ago.

They didn't have common templates for the bodies. These were real stock cars. Take it on the track and take your chances. Sure, there were rules, but not like today. Not as many, and not where things are measured by thousandths of an inch. Consequently, one driver's car could be dramatically better than the second-best car in the field. What NASCAR was in the 1950s and early 1960s is barely recognizable as the same sport we see today.

That doesn't stop fans from comparing the old guys with the stars of this era. Some deserve to rank with the best of any era; some don't. If we had a time machine and could put them in a car today, how would they fare? We could ask the same question of today's stars. Could they have won on the dirt tracks of the past in cars that were souped-up versions of what came off the showroom floor?

I'm betting Tony Stewart would have felt right at home racing with the old-school heroes such as Tim Flock and Buck Baker, and I have little doubt some of the men listed below could have shown today's super celebrity Cup stars a thing or two.

So let's turn back the clock and see what some of the NASCAR pioneers accomplished and whether they rank with the best of the best.

The Most Overrated Yesteryear Driver
NED JARRETT

If we were talking about NASCAR broadcasters, Ned Jarrett would rate as the most underrated of all time, but when it comes to driving the race car, the first generation of the Jarrett clan in NASCAR had some limitations. This pains me to say because Ned's picture should be in the dictionary under the word gentleman. Honestly, people don't come any better than Ned Jarrett—a class individual and a kind man.

Jarrett can take pride in the fact that he won 50 races at NASCAR's highest level, good enough to tie for 10th on the career list with Junior Johnson. But the statistics tell us: Only two of Jarrett's 50 victories came on super speedways. Most of the other 48 wins were small tracks (half-mile or shorter) and dirt tracks.

Some people might say the car had quite a bit to do with his only victory in the Southern 500 at Darlington in 1965. Two contenders had major problems. Fred Lorenzen blew an engine, and Cale Yarborough crashed. That's all the help Jarrett needed to claim a runaway victory. He won the race by 14 laps (17.5 miles), which remains the largest margin of victory in Cup history. If any driver won a race today by 14 laps, the car would be taken to NASCAR's Research and Development Center and examined by a team of inspectors, piece by piece.

Jarrett won the championship in 1961 and 1965. He had one victory in 46 starts in 1961. He also failed to finish 11 times but posted 34 top-10 finishes in the 46 races he entered. That means he finished in the top 10 every

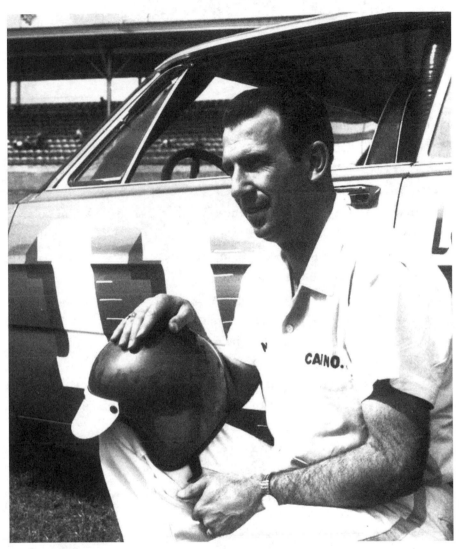

Driver Ned Jarrett, 32, of Camden, New Jersey, in 1965. (AP Photo)

time but once when his car was running at the end. He also had 23 top-5 finishes that year, but he took the checkered flag only once. It seems like a guy could have lucked into at least three of four wins if he had 23 top-5 finishes.

Jarrett's second championship in 1965 was more impressive with 13 victories, but Jarrett quit a year later at 34 years old. He was in the running for a third title when Ford announced it was withdrawing from NASCAR, so

Jarrett decided to retire, the only man in history to retire as a reigning champion.

Maybe things would have looked differently had Jarrett continued to race in his prime years. Maybe not.

Jarrett was a heck of a short-track racer. Forty-seven of his victories came on tracks half a mile or shorter, including 16 on tracks that were one-third of a mile or smaller. Jarrett had 33 victories on dirt tracks, but the big ovals were his weakness. Jarrett was winless in 20 Cup-level starts at Daytona. He was 0-for-15 on the 1.5-mile oval at Charlotte.

Jarrett won once in 15 starts on the 1.3-mile egg-shaped Darlington oval and was 1-for-14 on the 1.5-mile Atlanta track. Jarrett was also winless in three starts on the 1-mile Rockingham, North Carolina, oval. Jarrett never won a race on a road course.

That's what I mean by limitations. Some tracks didn't play to his strengths. He made sure that didn't happen for his son, however. Winning at the big tracks wasn't a problem one generation later.

Dale Jarrett's strength was winning on super speedways. Of his 32 Cup victories, 23 came on tracks larger than a mile. He won twice on Talladega's 2.66-mile oval and four times on the 2.5-mile Daytona oval. Jarrett also won four times on the 2-mile oval at Michigan.

Ned didn't get the chance to compete in as many big-track events as his son, but when Ned was on the big ovals, he rarely found a way to win.

Both Ned and Dale will make it into the new NASCAR Hall of Fame soon after it opens in 2010, but Dale's one championship and 32 victories is a more impressive effort than Ned's two championships and 50 wins. Dale did it against tougher competition at faster tracks in bigger events.

Dale's broadcasting career started in 2008, and it's clear he has the family genes in the booth—but the old man still has him beat there.

The Rest of the Top Five
2. BILL REXFORD

He won the 1950 NASCAR championship, the league's first full season, so many people view him highly. He posted his only win on May 30 of that year in Canfield, Ohio. It was also the site of his only pole one year later, yet he failed to lead a lap that season. So in 36 career starts, he had one pole and one victory. Rexford led 80 laps in his one victory. He led 18 laps the rest of his career, which spanned only five seasons.

Rexford beat Fireball Roberts for the 1950 title by 111 points, but Roberts made eight fewer starts (nine compared to 17 for Rexford). The only driver who made as many starts as Rexford was Lee Petty, who finished third in the standings despite posting five more top-5 finishes (nine to five) and two more top-10 finishes (13 to 11).

Aside from the inaugural 1949 NASCAR season when only eight sanctioned races took place, Rexford's 1950 crown, and his one victory, is as overrated as it gets.

3. LAKE SPEED

Too bad we're not rating names. Speed would certainly go down as a top-5 guy on the underrated side for that one, right behind Dick Trickle and Dick Passwater. But Lake's last name didn't work out so well on the track. He had one victory (the Darlington spring race in 1988) in 402 starts over 19 seasons. Speed was winless in his last 10 seasons.

Speed's stats aren't so hot, but that's true for a lot of guys who didn't make this list. The difference is many people had high expectation for Speed's career. He had his moments, but they didn't happen often enough for Speed to escape the overrated category.

He posted a top-5 finish in only one year of the last nine he competed, totaling a meager 16 for his career. I'll admit the man didn't have the best equipment to work with. He never won a pole and his average starting spot was 21st.

Some of his stats are painful to relive. In his final two seasons, Speed made 41 starts, and he didn't have a top-10 finish. Out of the 12,304 laps he raced in 1997 and 1998, Speed led only three laps.

Speed is definitely one of the best guys that ever sat in a race car. Lake and his wife, Rice, are on the board of directors of the Christian organization Motor Racing Outreach. Speed is well liked by almost everyone who knows him, both inside and outside of NASCAR.

4. GREG SACKS

Sacks' career elevates in the eyes of some folks because they remember him for his victory in the 1985 Firecracker 400 at Daytona. Sacks continued to race in all or part of 15 more Cup seasons without seeing Victory Lane again.

He only had two other top-5 finishes in his career, both in 1990, and he raced in 134 more Cup events without posting a top 5. Sacks didn't have a top 10 in his last 75 Cup events. He had some pretty sorry rides, but his average finish was four spots lower than where he started (27th compared to 23rd on the starting grid).

5. COO COO MARLIN

He could join those guys I listed above on the top-5 underrated names team. Coo Coo was quite the character but not the world's greatest driver. Marlin made 165 starts without winning a race and posted only nine top-5 finishes. He never finished second, and led only 105 laps out of the 34,726 he completed.

Marlin was decent at the big tracks. He finished fourth at Daytona on two occasions—the 1972 Firecracker 400 and the 1977 Daytona 500. That skill carried over to son Sterling, who won the Daytona 500 twice.

Coo Coo was victorious once at Daytona, winning a qualifying race for the 1973 Daytona 500. Sorry, but that didn't count as a real win. And, for the record, his real name was Clifton.

Most Underrated Yesteryear Driver
JUNIOR JOHNSON

Here's all you need to know about Junior: He completed 51,988 laps in his career and led 12,651 of them, an incredible 24 percent.

Richard Petty led 17 percent of the laps he completed. Midway through the 2008 season, Jeff Gordon had led 13 percent of his Cup laps. The great Dale Earnhardt only led 12.7 percent of the laps he finished. Even David Pearson, who I listed among the most underrated drivers of all time, led 18.8 percent of the laps he ran.

Junior Johnson peers from his car after winning the pole position for the Dixie 400 stock car race at the Atlanta International Raceway, on June 3, 1964. Johnson qualified for the $56,000 race with a four-lap speed of 145.906 mph. (AP photo)

It takes more than just leading laps to make the top of the underrated list. But clearly Johnson was something special in more ways than one. He was the old moonshiner who went to prison for a year and overcame his status as an ex-con to become one of the legendary figures in NASCAR history.

Johnson is one of only 11 drivers to post 50 victories in his career—and 45 of them came in an eight-season span from 1958-65 after returning from his stint in the big house. Johnson said he never thought he would see the day when his moonshine would have a place in NASCAR, but that day came in the 2008 Daytona 500. More on that later.

Johnson never won a championship because he never competed in all of the races. Johnson was a short-track master, but he could also get it done on some of the biggest, baddest, and fastest tracks. Johnson won the 1960 Daytona 500. He also won the 1963 Dixie 400 on the 1.5-mile oval at Atlanta and the 1965 Rebel 300 at Darlington.

Johnson' legacy in NASCAR goes far beyond his driving skills. The man almost single-handedly brought R.J. Reynolds and Winston to Cup as the title sponsor, transforming the sport and elevating NASCAR to a plateau it never would have achieved without corporate involvement.

Johnson also became one of NASCAR's greatest team owners. His drivers won six championships and 139 races, but his achievements outside the race car sometimes cause fans to forget what an outstanding racer he was.

Only seven seasons in his career did Johnson compete in more than half the races on the circuit. He won five or more races in six of those years. In 1965, the last season he competed as a Cup regular, Johnson led an astonishing 56 percent of the laps he completed, an unimaginable total by today's standards.

Johnson was back at Daytona in 2008, this time as a primary sponsor of a car. More than 50 years after doing time for brewing a little white lightning, Johnson's old moonshine recipe became an official part of the sport. Johnson's *Midnight Moon*, a legal and refined rendition of his old rot gut, was the sponsor on Jeremy Mayfield's car for the Daytona 500. "NASCAR used to run from the moonshine," Johnson told me at Daytona. "Now they run to it."

Johnson went into business with Piedmont Distillers to make a new version of his family's original moonshine. It's been a huge success. *Midnight Moon* is sold in 13 states, including Florida. "It's something I'm really proud of," Johnson said. "I've had a lot of offers from distilleries over the years, but I finally found one that gave me control."

Johnson wanted to keep as much of the original moonshine process as possible in the legal version. "We started with my dad's old recipe and cleaned it up a lot," he said. "It's made the same way, but we triple-stilled it and that took all the impurities out of it. The impurities were making it like gasoline. But we dropped the proof to 80 proof. That made it a more drinkable drink than the old 105 proof stuff."

Johnson decided to sponsor Mayfield's car at Daytona to help with the marketing campaign in Florida. "We're going to Texas next," Johnson said. "We hunt the states that drink the most liquor. It's going great. Sales are way ahead of anything that's ever come on the market."

Johnson, who is 77 now, said it felt great to be back at Daytona. Having a little moonshine around made it even better.

The Rest of the Top Five
2. LEEROY YARBROUGH

He never raced a full season of Cup competition, but he made the most of it when he was on the track. Yarbrough won only 14 races, but 12 of those victories came over a five-year span from 1966-70. He was at his best in the big events.

Yarbrough's shining season came in 1969 when he won both Daytona races and both events at Darlington, a year where he won seven times while driving for Junior Johnson. It was one of only two times when Yarbrough raced more than half the events in a season.

It was also the year Yarbrough became the first driver to win what was known as NASCAR's Triple Crown, claiming victories in the Daytona 500, the Southern 500, and the World 600 in Charlotte that season. Yarbrough still raced only 30 of 54 events in 1969, posting 16 top-5 finishes and 21 top-10 finishes. He finished a so-so 16th in the standings only because he missed 24 races.

He was at his best on the high-banked ovals, winning three times at Charlotte and twice at Atlanta. It's too bad Yarbrough never ran a full season. Only twice in his career did he race more than half the events in a year. From 1966-70, Yarbrough posted 44 top-5 finishes in just 99 starts.

3. HERSHEL MCGRIFF

The man should win an award for competing over a 44-year span on and off from 1950 to 1993. He raced in the Cup road race at Sonoma when he was 65, completing 27 laps before he blew an engine. His remarkable career was much more than just longevity, McGriff knew what to do in a race car.

The 1954 season was the only time McGriff raced in more than five events for the year, and he won four times in 24 starts. He also had 17 top-10 finishes that season and five poles. McGriff won four of the last nine races that season. McGriff was 26 years old at the time, but he didn't race at the Cup level again until 1971 when he was 43.

Before the 1955 season, McGriff was offered the driving duties for a new team formed by Carl Kiekhaefer, but McGriff decided to stay home in Oregon to guide his growing business in the timber mill industry. Tim Flock was the second choice for Kiekhaefer. Flock won 18 races that season and claimed his second championship.

McGriff returned for three races in 1971 and competed in only four races the following year, but finished in the top 6 three times. His worst finish was 12th. All of his wins came on short tracks, but he finished fifth in the 1973 Daytona 500, one of only three races he competed in that season. He also finished fifth on the two-mile super speedway at College Station, Texas, in 1972.

Obviously, the man missed his prime years for racing, but his accomplishments earned him a spot on NASCAR's list of 50 Greatest Drivers.

4. FIREBALL ROBERTS

He raced in more than half the events only twice in his career. In 1950, he competed in only nine of 19 races but finished second in the standings, only 111 points behind series champion Bill Rexford, who competed in 17 events.

"Fireball was way ahead of his time," said NASCAR vice president and historian Jim Hunter. "He was at his best in the biggest races. His concentration level seemed to go up at places like Daytona and Darlington. He was sort of like the Reggie Jackson of racing because he made his name at the major events the way Reggie always did in the World Series."

I listed some of those accomplishments in naming Roberts No. 3 on the most underrated Daytona 500 winners, but his underrated status goes beyond one event.

"Fireball was a pretty rough character in his day," Hunter said. "But he also was a professional. He was even a spokesman for Falstaff beer. I can't think of another driver at the time [who] had endorsements."

Whether on the track or off, Roberts made the most of his abilities. He finished in the top 5 in 93 of 206 starts, an impressive 45 percent of the time. It compares favorably with the best drivers in NASCAR history. Richard Petty posted top-5 finishes 47 percent of the time. At the end of 2007, Jeff Gordon had top-5 finishes in 46 percent of his Cup starts.

Roberts was only 35 when a crash in the 1964 World 600 caused injuries that would take his life a few weeks later.

5. JOE WEATHERLY

He raced a full season just twice in his career and won the championship both times—and it happened after he turned 40. Weatherly won back-to-back championship in 1962-63 when he was 40 and 41 years old. He won nine races in 1961 when he only raced in 25 events, posting 14 top-5 finishes. Weatherly had 45 top-10 finishes in 52 starts for the 1962 season.

Weatherly spent most of his early career racing in other divisions. He won 101 races over a two-year span (1952-53) in the NASCAR modified division. He also won 12 times over four seasons in the convertible series. Weatherly won three American Motorcycle Association championships before he began racing stock cars.

Weatherly's driving style was simple—all out on every lap. The man wrecked a lot of cars and blew a lot of engines when he wasn't winning, something his team owners didn't appreciate at times.

The most amazing accomplishment regarding his 1963 championship was that it came while racing for nine different team owners. Just think about that. Try winning a Cup title today with just two different team owners. No chance.

Along with his racing skills, Weatherly was quite a character. He was known as the Clown Prince of Stock Car Racing. Weatherly and Curtis

Turner were blacklisted by rental car companies for racing each other and tearing up the cars. That story was the inspiration for a famous scene in the move *Days of Thunder* when Cole Trickle (Tom Cruise) and Rowdy Burns (Michael Rooker) trade paint in their rental cars.

Weatherly was racing at his best in NASCAR when he was killed in an accident at Riverside, California, in the fifth race of 1964. Weatherly's head came outside the car as it hit a retaining wall. That accident led to NASCAR mandating window netting to keep a driver's head inside the vehicle.

Weatherly is the only driver killed on the track while defending his title. Alan Kulwicki's death came the season after his 1992 championship, but he lost his life in a plane crash.

One-Win Wonders

As of July 2008, NASCAR has had 55 drivers who won once in Cup and never accomplished the feat again. I am excluding active drivers for the obvious reason that they can still work their way off of the list. Believe it or not, not everyone who only posted one victory is overrated. It all depends on how many chances they had and where they won.

For many of them, it's amazing they found a way to win once. For others, one victory is reflective of how good they really were. Here's a few that stand out.

Most Overrated One-Win Wonder
RICHARD BRICKHOUSE

He won the inaugural Cup race at Talladega, but most of the best drivers weren't there. The enormous track was known as Alabama International Motor Speedway when it opened as the biggest and fastest oval track in the world. The 1969 Talladega 500 was the first and only boycott by NASCAR drivers, as 37 of the regular Cup competitors refused to race in the event.

The drivers felt the tires could not withstand speeds that were approaching 200 mph on the 2.66-mile high-banked oval. Tires were coming apart in practice after only four or five laps. But Big Bill France saw other reasons for the boycott threat. A drivers' union known as the Professional Drivers Association formed a few weeks earlier. Richard Petty was elected the president of the PDA. France wasn't about to give in to any union demands.

Neither side was giving in, so the top drivers packed up and left. Petty, Cale Yarborough, Bobby Allison, LeeRoy Yarbrough, David Pearson, and Buddy Baker were among the boycotters. "I hate to do this," Baker reportedly said as he departed. "But I like me. I've grown accustomed to living." Ironically, one year later at Talladega, Baker became the first driver to top 200 on a closed course.

Brickhouse was no Buddy Baker. He was a 29-year-old North Carolina racer who broke with the union to compete in the race. France managed to fill the field with replacement drivers and cars, including some Grand Touring sports cars and ARCA cars. The starting grid still had a few quality racers like Bobby Isaac and Tiny Lund, along with Buck Baker, Buddy's dad who was near the end of his career. The starting lineup even included two doctors.

Also racing that day was Richard Childress, who finished 23rd in the first Cup race of his career. Seventeen years later, he was the team owner for Dale Earnhardt as they won the first of six championships together. But Childress was no competition on the race track that September day at Talladega in 1969.

Calling this a race is a bit of a stretch. Most of the event was run at a reduced pace of 175 mph, even though the cars could have gone almost 25 mph faster. A caution flag was thrown about every 25 laps—officially for debris and unofficially to change the tires.

Brickhouse dropped the hammer on the throttle in the final 10 laps and easily won the race by seven seconds. Brickhouse never raced full time in the series and never received another freebie into Victory Lane.

The Rest of the Top Five
2. LARRY FRANK

He wasn't the man who took the checkered flag, but Frank went into the record book as the winner of the 1962 Southern 500 at Darlington. The fans exited the grounds believing that Junior Johnson had won the race, but five hours after it ended, NASCAR officials declared Frank the winner after checking the scoring cards.

It was a lot tougher to keep track of that stuff in the old days, especially in a four-hour event with 364 laps. The decision to announce Frank as the winner didn't happen until almost midnight, so most of the newspapers and TV stations didn't have the information until the next day.

It led to one of the great leads ever by the late Bloys Britt of the Associated Press. In Victory Lane, Johnson said he would use his prize money to build some new chicken houses on his farm. After Britt learned Frank had won, Blatt wrote this zinger: "Junior counted his chicken houses before they hatched."

3. BOBBY HILLIN

Like Brickhouse, the next three drivers on this list had their one big moment of glory at Talladega. Something about the red clay of Alabama brought out the best in these guys. The only victory for each of them came off the giant Alabama oval in the days before restrictor plates were added.

Teenage Bobby was considered the original young gun. The Midland, Texas, product started Cup racing at 18 years old, and almost everyone in NASCAR expected big things were headed his way. It never quite worked out except for that one Alabama moment when he held off Tim Richmond to win in 1986. Hillin was only 22, the youngest winner ever at that point.

It was all downhill from there, as he raced 11 more seasons without winning. Hillin posted four top-5 finishes in 1986, then only four more the rest of his career. Hillin didn't have a top-5 finish in his last 146 races, and he earned only four top-10 finishes during that span. He led only 21 laps in the final seven years of his career.

4. RON BOUCHARD

Another Talladega wonder, he won in his 11th Cup start as a rookie in 1981. After that, it was zero for the next 149 starts before calling it quits. He led 224 laps of the 42,884 he logged in races. That's one half of one percent.

Bouchard led only six laps the day he won at Dega, but he led the one that counted. Darrell Waltrip and Terry Labonte were battling for the win on the last lap and completely forgot about Bouchard, who scooted down low and raced past both of them coming to the checkered flag.

It was a three-way photo finish at the line. Waltrip couldn't believe it, thinking Bouchard was a lap down. "Where the heck did he come from?" Waltrip asked afterward.

5. DICK BROOKS

His golden moment came at Talladega in 1973, winning a race where only 26 of 50 starters still were on the track at the end. That was it for Brooks in 358 Cup starts. He should have posted a few more victories because he finished in the top 10 almost half the time (150 races). Brooks also compiled 57 top-5 finishes. How do you race near the front that often and only win once?

Brooks later became a highly respected radio broadcaster (a place where he was definitely underrated) calling NASCAR events for MRN Radio in the 1990s. He was also known for wearing blue jean overalls for the broadcast. Brooks passed away in 2006 at age 63, two weeks before the Daytona 500.

Most Underrated One-Win Wonder
MARIO ANDRETTI

His one victory was the 1967 Daytona 500. If you're going to Victory Lane only one time in a NASCAR event, that's the place to do it. Andretti made only 14 Cup starts during four seasons, moonlighting while becoming one of the greatest open-wheel racers in history.

Andretti beat some of the giants of racing in his Daytona victory, including Richard Petty, David Pearson, A.J. Foyt, Bobby Allison, and Buddy Baker, to name a few. What Andretti and Foyt did as open-wheelers in NASCAR seems even more remarkable today because we've seen how difficult it has been for the current crop of open-wheel guys to win in NASCAR, even after moving to Cup full time.

Three-time IndyCar Series champ Sam Hornish Jr., Indy car veteran Patrick Carpentier, and 2007 Indy 500 winner Dario Franchitti struggled just to finish in the top 30 at most events in 2008. Former Formula One

Mario Andretti holds up his trophy with his wife by his side after he won the Daytona 500 on February 26, 1967, at Daytona Beach, Florida. He finished the 200-lap race driving a 1967 Ford. (AP Photo)

driver Juan Pablo Montoya, the 2000 Indy 500 winner, won at Sonoma in his rookie season in 2007, but he hasn't set the Cup world on fire in two seasons of NASCAR racing.

None of those drivers had the equipment Andretti and Foyt had when they won in NASCAR, but these were drivers who just showed up for a one-off here and there and won some of the biggest events in the sport.

Even if they had Jeff Gordon's car, I don't think any of the current open-wheel guys in NASCAR are going to step into a win the Daytona 500.

The Rest of the Top Five
2. WENDELL SCOTT

His one win made racing history as he was the first black driver to win in NASCAR. It happened more than 40 years ago and has yet to be equaled. Scott won on the half-mile dirt track at Speedway Park in Jacksonville, Florida. It was his shining moment in a 13-year career that included 147 top-10 finishes in 495 starts. Scott finished in the top 10 in the standings for four consecutive years (1966-69).

NASCAR does not have an African American driver in Cup today. Scott's achievements more than four decades ago came at many tracks in the Southeast during the highly volatile times of the Civil Rights era. That alone makes his achievement worthy of praise.

3. MARVIN BURKE

This is an easy one. Burke won the NASCAR event on the .625-mile dirt oval and Oakland Stadium in California on October 14, 1951.

No big deal, you say? Wrong. That also happened to be Burke's only race. It was one and done. Nothing like going out on top—Burke did his thing and left at age 33. He led 156 of the 400 laps and took home a whopping paycheck of $1,875.

Here's a funny thing about that win: There were two other NASCAR events on the same day. One at Shippenville, Pennsylvania, that was won by Tim Flock, and one at Martinsville, Virginia, that Frank Mundy won. Flock finished third in the championship that year and Mundy was fifth. Had either of them decided to go across the country that day, maybe Burke would have ended his career 0-for-1.

However, the field at Oakland had some top drivers, including Tim's brother, Fonty Flock. Fonty finished second in the 1951 season standings but settled for 11th that afternoon in California. Marvin Panch, winner of the 1961 Daytona 500, was competing in his first NASCAR event that day. He finished sixth.

4. MARK DONOHUE

The Indy-car racer competed only six times in NASCAR over two seasons (1972-73) but won the Riverside, California, road race in 1973 while driving for Roger Penske. It was Penske's first NASCAR win.

Donohue was the last non-regular driver (or road-course ringer, as we call them today) to win a Cup road race. In four of Donohue's six career starts, his car had a mechanical failure, so he won two of the three races that he actually finished.

5. DANNY GRAVES

The Modesto, California, driver only competed in nine NASCAR events, all on the West Coast in 1957-58. He won at Sacramento in '57, but that isn't what stands out.

Graves' car had a mechanical failure in six of the nine races he ran. But he finished in the top 5 in all three races when he was still running at the end. The man even managed to finish ninth in a race at Bremerton, Washington, when his engine blew with six laps to go.

CHAPTER 10

Claims and Concepts

If you say something long enough and loud enough, people will believe it. NASCAR makes a few claims that many people accept as fact, but a closer look shows some of those accepted truths aren't quite as cut-and-dried as they appear.

Just how many fans does NASCAR have? Does most of the field have an equal chance of winning? Does sponsor exclusivity really work? Is more always better when it comes to the number of races on the schedule?

NASCAR is also missing a couple of concepts that could improve things overall. Money piles up quickly in this sport, going out as fast as it comes in. What's it all really worth? Franchising teams could make it all worth a lot more.

Drivers are worth more today than ever in the history of racing, but they don't view themselves as valuable commodities, as in valuing their lives. Courage in racing is an admirable thing. Foolishness is not.

Check out the details, and see what I mean.

Most Overrated Claim
NASCAR'S 75 MILLION FANS

NASCAR has claimed for years that 75 million of us are fans, roughly one out of four Americans. Well, that's quite a number. Let's see now. Going by that logic, Auto Club Speedway in Fontana, California, shouldn't have any trouble selling all 90,000 grandstand seats. There are 13 million people in the metropolitan area of Los Angeles, so that means 3.25 million of them are NASCAR fans—can't seem to find them come race day, however.

If NASCAR's figures are correct, more than 400,000 people in Manhattan are also NASCAR fans. That's 25 percent of the 1.6 million people who live among the mass of humanity on that island. Funny thing, though. I bet they are awfully hard to find. I made light of this lofty number two years ago while in New York City for the Cup Awards Banquet.

Just on a hunch, I assumed a quick survey might fail to produce that one-in-four percentage of NASCAR followers scurrying about Times Square or Central Park. But I had no desire to stand on a corner at Rockefeller Center and ask folks who walked by if they were NASCAR fans. Even excluding the ones who glared at or cursed me, I seriously doubt four of 10 would claim a membership in the NASCAR Nation. Four of 100 is a more reasonable estimate, even on a week when NASCAR's stars were in town.

Several thousand fans showed up for the annual Victory Lap ceremony at Times Square that week, but don't be misled—watching a parade doesn't make you a fan. Three out of four are probably Yankees fans. No doubt most of them are New York Giants fans. But NASCAR fans? Don't think so.

Clearly, I'm having fun with NASCAR's silly number because New York City and Los Angeles are not the places to fairly debunk the total. What if I did the same survey in downtown Charlotte? The positive response would probably top 50 percent, but we're talking nationwide. To say 25 percent of the diverse make-up of people in the USA are NASCAR fans just doesn't add up.

NASCAR has millions of fans, and the numbers have gone up dramatically over the last 10 years. Attendance increased 28 percent from 1996 to 2005. A downward trend in the economy caused attendance to drop at many tracks in 2008, but most Cup events still draw more than 100,000 fans, or sellout crowds if the facility has less than 100,000 seats.

Sales of NASCAR merchandise skyrocketed over the 10-year span, from $600 million in 1996 to $2.2 billion in 2006. As those numbers rose, which were verifiable figures, 75 million became the accepted number when discussing NASCAR fandom without anyone really questioning its validity.

Anne Finucane, chief marketing officer for Bank of America, used that figure in December 2007 while announcing a new partnership as the official bank of NASCAR. Kerry Tharp, NASCAR's director of public relations, said the claim of 75 million fans is easily explained. "The figure means that 75 million people indicated they follow the sport in one form or another," Tharp said.

That's a very broad statement. What's the criteria? A person knows who Dale Earnhardt Jr. is? They were flipping channels and watched a NASCAR race for 10 laps? NASCAR's research lists five categories to get to the 75 million mark. The top two categories—avid fans and serious fans—account for 41 million. It's the other 34 million that gets a little iffy.

About 15 million of the total is listed as general sports fans who follow NASCAR but aren't passionate about it. Then there are 10 million more considered passive TV fans, such as people who watch broadcasts of races but don't follow the sport in other ways.

But the biggest stretch of the "NASCAR fan" moniker is another nine million categorized as uninvolved TV fans, people who sometimes watch races. You have to wonder how many in those bottom two categories are paying attention to the sport.

The Daytona 500, NASCAR's premiere event, had an 11.3 Nielsen rating in 2007. It was the highest TV rating in NASCAR history. That rating equals about 37 million viewers. So only half of the fan base watched the biggest event of the year? Where were the other 38 million fans? That was never a realistic figure.

Veteran driver Mark Martin thinks people spend too much time trying to evaluate numbers. He knows what he sees now is a huge difference from 1982, the first time he attended NASCAR's awards banquet in New York. "Everywhere I go and every function and every race, the response is bigger than ever before, including New York," Martin said.

NASCAR has tons of loyal fans from New York to Hawaii, but 75 million of them? Not yet.

Overrated Claim No. 2
PARITY

One of the things NASCAR wants most is a level playing field. It's the idea that anyone has a chance to win on any given weekend. Well, parity lovers, don't hold your breath on that one. The truth is that most of the drivers on the starting grid for each Sprint Cup race have little or no chance of winning that event. Some don't have good enough equipment, some don't have the skill or the experience to get it done, and some just haven't had much luck in a particular season.

Only 16 of the top 43 drivers in the 2007 standings went to Victory Lane. Twenty-seven of them didn't take a checkered flag, which is 63 percent of the field. Only 13 of the top 43 won a race in 2006 and 2004. The 2005 season had 15 winners. Two drivers won 16 of 36 events in 2007. Jimmie Johnson had 10 victories, and Jeff Gordon had six. Only four other drivers earned multiple wins—three for Stewart and Carl Edwards and two for Matt Kenseth and Kurt Busch.

For some teams—Petty Enterprises, Michael Waltrip Racing, Bill Davis Racing, Haas CNC Racing (maybe in 2009 with Tony Stewart as an owner/driver), Hall of Fame Racing, Robby Gordon Motorsports, Wood Brothers Racing, Yates Racing—winning wasn't a realistic option in 2007. Those teams account for 13 drivers in the field most weeks.

Things got worse in 2008. Heading into the Allstate 400 at the Brickyard, the second biggest event of the season and the 20th race of the year, 33 of the 43 starters were winless for the season. That's 77 percent of the field who hadn't been to Victory Lane in 2008.

Three drivers who have won in the past—Elliott Sadler, Casey Mears, and Jamie McMurray—didn't appear capable of winning at that event. They hadn't run well all season. They didn't win at Indy. Four other drivers in the top 35 at Indy (guaranteeing a starting spot) weren't racing at a winning level—Sam Hornish Jr., Reed Sorenson, Regan Smith, and Paul Menard. They were inexperienced NASCAR drivers still learning their craft in their stock cars.

None of the drivers who rank outside the top 35 (and have to qualify on speed) heading into Indy had any shot at winning, including Joe Nemechek,

A.J. Allmendinger, and Patrick Carpentier. Nemechek didn't have the equipment, Allmendinger and Carpentier didn't have enough experience.

Of all the starters for the 2008 Allstate 400, at least 23 had virtually no chance of winning. Even five drivers inside the Chase cutoff—Jeff Gordon, Tony Stewart, Kevin Harvick, Greg Biffle, and Matt Kenseth—had not won in 2008 entering the July race at the Brickyard. That trend continued at Indy. Kyle Busch, who dominated the circuit with seven victories in the first 19 races, accounted in large part for their dry spell.

Even among the 2008 winners heading into the Allstate 400, going to Victory Lane is a rare treat. Only three drivers had more than one victory at that point—Busch (seven), Carl Edwards (three), and Kasey Kahne (two). Jimmie Johnson earned his second victory of the season at the Brickyard.

Many people assume NASCAR has more parity than major open-wheel leagues. Midway through 2008, the IndyCar Series actually had a better

Kyle Busch celebrates in victory lane after winning the NASCAR Sprint Cup Best Buy 400 auto race on Sunday, June 1, 2008, at Dover International Speedway in Dover, Delaware. He dominated early in 2008, winning seven of the first 19 races. (AP Photo/Russ Hamilton)

percentage of winners considering the numbers of races run and the total numbers of cars in each event.

The Sprint Cup Series had 10 different winners in 19 events among a starting grid of 43 competitors heading to the Allstate 400 in 2008. IndyCar had eight different winners in 13 races among an average starting grid of 25 drivers.

Even Formula One compared well with Cup (percentage wise) midway through 2008 for the number of winners. Almost everyone views F1 as a series in which only a select few can win, but F1 had four different winners in July in 10 races among 20 drivers. So 25 percent of the drivers in F1 had won, compared to 23 percent in Cup for almost twice the number of races.

More teams and more drivers have a chance of winning in Cup than F1, and Cup is still a series in which the biggest teams with the most money win most of the time while everyone else just makes laps.

Most Overrated Number
36-RACE CUP SCHEDULE

Make that 38 weekends when you add in the two All-Star events, and that doesn't include test sessions. Sprint Cup is the longest season in professional sports. It starts with the Daytona 500 festivities in early February and ends the third week of November with the Chase finale event at Homestead-Miami Speedway.

That schedule has only three off weekends over a 41-week span. It's an enormous strain, particularly on the crews more than the drivers. It has also reached the point of over-saturation. The truth is that NASCAR grew too big too fast. Giant facilities with more than 150,000 seats became harder to fill in 2008 due to higher ticket prices and difficult economic times, including soaring gas prices.

It's all about supply and demand. The supply of 36 Cup events each year is too much for the demand. No other major racing series comes close to 36 races. Formula One had 18 races in 2008. The newly merged IndyCar Series had 19, including the final Champ Car event in Long Beach and the exhibition race in Australia. The IndyCar Series will stage 18 events in 2009.

Even the NFL, the other major U.S. sport that stages games on a weekly basis, doesn't have as many games as NASCAR has Cup events. A team that plays five preseason games (most play four) would only play a maximum of 25 games if it made it to the Super Bowl.

There were many years when NASCAR's Grand National Series (what Cup is today) raced more than 36 events, 20 of 21 years between 1951 and 1971. That includes a 62-race schedule in 1964. Fifty-six of those races took place over an eight-state area in the Southeast, and three times that season NASCAR ran three races over a three-day span. However, no one raced all 62 events and only seven drivers raced more than 50 events.

Comparing that to what drivers and teams do today is preposterous. The 36-race schedule today crisscrosses the country several times and is far more demanding than the 50- and 60-race schedule before the modern era began in 1972.

Shortening today's schedule to 30 events would make the season less of a grind on all of the teams. It would also increase the demand for tickets if races were dropped at tracks that have a difficult time filling most of the seats for two events—Atlanta, Auto Club Speedway, Lowe's Motor Speedway, and Michigan, to name a few. It also wouldn't hurt to cut a race from places where sponsors don't want to go twice, like Pocono and Martinsville.

There it is. We've just cut the schedule to 30 races and made things better for everyone. So will it happen? Not a chance in you know where. No track wants to give up a Cup date. It's a gigantic cash cow (at least $20 million per event) even if you don't sell all the seats. NASCAR also has contractual obligations that make the idea almost impossible to accomplish.

Television networks agree to pay NASCAR hundreds of millions of dollars based on televising a certain number of events. Reducing that number would mean a reduction in the amount of money the networks agreed to pay. NASCAR reached a new eight-year television agreement worth $4.48 billion, which started in 2007. The new deal brought ABC/ESPN back into the sport after a six-year absence.

Track owners receive 65 percent of TV revenues, team owners receive 25 percent, and NASCAR keeps 10 percent—any track that lost a date would suffer a double whammy in reduced revenue.

Sprint also pays $70 million a year as the title sponsor based on the 36-race schedule. If the schedule was cut back to 30 races, the Sprint executives might insist on cutting their payment by the same percentage, down to around $58 million.

For better or worse, the grueling 36-race schedule won't get smaller anytime soon.

Most Overrated Concept
SPONSOR EXCLUSIVITY

Big money from sponsors is what it's all about to compete at the Cup level. But some companies are being told to take their cash and go home. As stated earlier, NASCAR receives $70 million a year from Sprint (formerly Nextel) for title sponsorship of the Cup Series. But the exclusivity rights

Jeff Burton at the NASCAR Nextel Cup Sharp Aquos 500 at the California Speedway in Fontana, California, on Sunday, September 2, 2007. The sponsor logos were removed because the AT&T/Cingular sponsorship conflicted with Sprint's exclusivity agreement. A lawsuit was settled out of court, and the AT&T logos were eventually restored. (AP Photo/Francis Specker)

that come with it have kept some competing telecommunications companies from staying in Cup or even entering the series.

AT&T took legal action against Sprint and NASCAR in 2007 for the rights to place its logo on Jeff Burton's No. 31 Chevrolet. Burton's Cingular sponsorship was grandfathered in when Sprint/Nextel signed its deal with NASCAR to replace Winston as the title sponsor in 2004. But the AT&T merger with Cingular ended the Cingular brand name. NASCAR officials said AT&T was not allowed to change the logos on Burton's car. AT&T filed a lawsuit and a federal judge issued an injunction in May 2007 allowing AT&T's logos back on the car.

That ruling was overturned by an appeals court in August 2007, causing Richard Childress Racing to race the car without logos for several events. Another injunction hearing was scheduled for September 18, but further legal action was avoided by a settlement a month later. The AT&T logos were back on Burton's car for the Richmond race on September 8, 2007, after Sprint and AT&T reached an agreement to allow AT&T to continue as the primary sponsor of the car through the end of the 2008 season.

But it meant RCR officials had to go to work to find a new sponsor for Burton to start 2009. The teams announced in July 2008 that Caterpillar would sponsor Burton's car in 2009, thus leaving Bill Davis Racing, where it had been the primary sponsor for Dave Blaney and the No. 22 Toyota.

The exclusivity agreement cost NASCAR a major sponsor and left one team looking for a new company to pay the bills.

The same thing happened to Penske Racing in 2008 after Verizon bought out Alltel, which was grandfathered in as Ryan Newman's sponsor of the No. 12 Dodge. NASCAR informed Roger Penske that he couldn't switch the car to the Verizon logo. This came at a time when Penske was negotiating a new contract for Newman.

Even though Penske said he could field the team without a primary sponsor (one of the few team owners wealthy enough to consider it), being in limbo on a primary sponsorship isn't something any potential driver wants to hear if he's considering signing with a team. NASCAR officials should have seen this coming when they signed a telecommunications group as the title sponsor. These companies swallow each other up every week. The irony of it is Sprint did the same thing to Nextel.

The days of one sponsor hanging around as the series name for 30 years, as R.J. Reynolds did with Winston, are long gone. So NASCAR should think carefully before agreeing to give title sponsors exclusivity, thus barring similar companies from participating in the sport. NASCAR says it balances out because part of that $70 million it gets from Sprint each year goes into the points fund paid to the drivers at the end of the season. It's a fair point, but the possibility of teams closing up shop because their potential sponsor can't play in the NASCAR sandbox is a dangerous situation.

Most Underrated Business Idea
FRANCHISING

Alan Kulwicki won the Winston Cup championship in 1992 with a sponsorship deal from Hooters worth $3 million. In 2008, it cost Sprint Cup teams more than that just to go testing each year. These days, $3 million is nothing more than pocket change for some organizations. Serious money is what it takes to run with the big boys in NASCAR today.

If you want your company's name on the car of one of the top drivers in the sport, you better have more than $15 million written down on a potential contract. That's what it takes just to consider becoming a primary sponsor for a full Cup season. For a name like Dale Earnhardt Jr., get ready to pony up twice that amount for a full season.

Today's sponsorship costs are causing many teams to use a combined sponsorship deal now, including Earnhardt's deal at Hendrick Motorsports. Amp Energy Drink and the National Guard split time on the No. 88 Chevy hood for an estimated $15 million each per year.

The primary sponsor is only part of the money train. Throw in associate sponsors, TV money, and contingency awards, and the figure skyrockets. It takes major bucks to play in NASCAR's pen, but it has become increasingly difficult for teams to get the funds they need to stay on the track. A struggling economy in 2008 brought major concerns for many teams in the Cup garage. Cup was starting to price itself outside what many corporations were willing to invest.

Even five years ago, I wrote that NASCAR was starting to look a little like Major League Baseball with a structure that includes the haves and the have-nots. Major teams with multi-million dollar sponsors—such as Hendrick Motorsports, Roush Fenway Racing, Joe Gibbs Racing, and Richard Childress Racing—have enormous operations with more than 400 employees. But smaller teams without big-dollar sponsors are struggling to get by.

Some of them, like Andy Petree and Travis Carter, quit trying in recent years. Petree, a championship crew chief for Dale Earnhardt before becoming a team owner, has moved on to a successful broadcasting career. Carter, who has been involved in NASCAR for more than 30 years, closed the doors on his two-car team in 2002 after the Kmart bankruptcy ended their sponsorship deal with his team. Teams have tried to protect themselves the last couple of years by bringing in financial partners and investment firms as co-owners of the operation. Even Petty Enterprises was forced to give financial control to a Boston investment firm.

Team owners have talked for years about becoming franchises to NASCAR, similar to the way big league teams are in the NFL, MLB, and the NBA. NASCAR has always balked at the suggestion, saying it works better having all the teams as independent contractors.

Driver Jeff Burton, one of the smartest guys in the sport, saw five years ago that the concept needed to change. "In the current structure, it isn't NASCAR's business how teams run their business," Burton said. "But that doesn't mean the current structure is the correct way to do it. It should mean something to keep the owners that have a huge investment in the sport. They should have some protection."

Burton was ahead of the curve in talking about franchising. "I think it's time for it," he told me for a 2003 *Dallas Morning News* story. "Franchises should be awarded, but you have to earn it by being competitive. If the owner isn't competitive enough, he would have to be at risk of losing his franchise." Burton thinks franchises would add value to each NASCAR team. As it stands now, a team's worth is based strictly on its parts and pieces. Burton made a specific analogy while he was still driving the No. 99 Ford for Jack Roush.

"Let's say we had franchises and Jack decided he wanted to sell," Burton said. "The 99 team would be worth a tremendous amount of money, just like an NFL team or an NBA team." In 2008, *Forbes* magazine listed the estimated worth of the top Cup teams. Hendrick Motorsports was No. 1 at $339 million for its four-car operation, which employs more than 500 people. Could Rick Hendrick sell it for that amount? The way it is now, if an owner decides he can't do it anymore, the only equity he has is in items that depreciate at such a rapid pace they mean nothing. His biggest investment is in people, which he can't sell.

Burton also believes franchise fees and rules could restrict teams and control costs. "I'm not sure how we would do it, but you could make it where there was a limited number of people they could employ," Burton said. "Or have a salary cap, which seems ridiculous for a driver to say, but if it's in the best interest of the sport, I'm OK with it." Burton realized at the time his plan was a futuristic idea at best, but it is more meaningful today than ever before.

Sometimes things cycle back. Here's an example.

"Certainly, we're interested in the overall health of the garage area," said NASCAR president Mike Helton. "But this is an economic issue that affects everyone. And the sport continues to grow. We've lost some sponsors, but we also have brought in some new sponsors. There certainly is room to have more sponsors. The exposure these teams get now is at an all-time high."

The funny thing about those comments is that Helton said them six years ago, but he could have said the exact same thing yesterday. Sponsor exposure has risen dramatically in recent years with NASCAR receiving increased coverage through more venues, including network television and Internet sites.

DuPont has been on the hood of Jeff Gordon's car since his rookie season in 1993. DuPont chairman Chad Holliday said in 2008 that his company's return on investment for the sponsorship the No. 24 Chevy is three to one. Three to one? Holy cash cow! DuPont is putting an estimated $20 million a year into Hendrick Motorsports, and the DuPont suits believe it generates $60 million in revenue.

Where do I sign? Let me sponsor one of these cars so I can get that kind of profit from it. But there's a catch—in my case, there's that little problem of not having the $20 million, but those who do face another dilemma. What you get from sponsoring Jeff Gordon is far better than sponsoring Dave Blaney. Gordon's car is shown on the tube a lot more than Blaney's ride. NASCAR estimates television exposure overall for corporate sponsors was worth more than $3 billion for one season.

One would think sponsors would jump at the opportunity to be involved with a Sprint Cup team, but the skyrocketing costs and slow economy have companies acting cautiously before investing. "I think our sport is extremely healthy," said Texas Motor Speedway president Eddie Gossage. "But at the same time, everyone involved has to be careful about making good business decisions and spending money wisely. The pool of companies that can invest $20 million a year is extremely limited."

Companies make sponsorship decisions based on many reasons. For example, it doesn't hurt to have the name Earnhardt if you're looking to make a deal. And some companies target races at specific markets where they have the most customers, so the company only wants to pick up the tab for that event.

Some people in NASCAR are alarmed at the explosion of costs over a short period of time. In 1998, most of the top teams in Cup were getting between $5 and $7 million for a primary sponsor. So costs have almost tripled in 10 years.

Franchising would help offset that increase and possibly begin bringing costs down, but Gossage said no one should shed any tears for Cup team owners. "Most of these Cup teams are making money," he said. "And team owners will spend all the money they have and then some. Then they'll complain they don't have any money, even though they have 727 jets parked at an airport by the track."

Most Underrated Emotion
FEAR

It's the word no driver wants to bring up, but one that should always have a place in the back of his mind. Fear. The fear factor is missing today in NASCAR. For all you super-macho types out there, that may sound like a manly thing. It's a stupid thing.

Many drivers today see themselves as bulletproof. They just don't believe they could get seriously hurt. That's a bad thing. With all the safety advancements over the last decade, a crash has become something that ends your day, not threatens your life. Drivers often walk away without a scratch. And we're all thankful the sport has reached that point of safety, but there is a dark side. The illusion of total safety causes some of the young drivers entering the sport to view racing in NASCAR like bumper cars at the county fair.

Aggressive driving is more prevalent that ever before because the possibility of getting hurt seems so remote. For some drivers, serious or fatal injuries were part of the old days, not something that happens today. Safety in NASCAR has progressed to the point where many drivers have a sense of invincibility.

Only 18 of the 43 drivers who started the 2008 Daytona 500 were in the field seven years earlier when Dale Earnhardt was killed. No one has lost his life in a Cup event since that tragic day. Serious injuries are almost non-existent. Many of the drivers in Cup now have never been involved in a race when a driver was killed, and some of them have never seen a driver seriously injured.

The S.A.F.E.R. barrier, head and neck restraints, carbon fiber seats, and the Car of Tomorrow have all played a part in revolutionizing safety in NASCAR. But that increased safety has also created a Superman mentality for some drivers, because bashing the sheet metal of another car doesn't often lead to any personal physical consequence. It's completely false logic, but many drivers haven't experienced anything to change that perception.

Other racing leagues have experienced fatalities more recently. NHRA Funny Car driver Scott Kalitta was killed in 2008, 15 months after Funny Car driver Eric Medlen lost his life in a testing accident at Gainesville, Florida. IndyCar Series driver Paul Dana was killed in 2006 during a practice session before the season-opening event at Miami. Those incidents don't hit home for NASCAR drivers, however, who feel it's more of a "that's them, not us" situation.

NASCAR has gone from the most dangerous form of racing to the safest in less than a decade. In the past, danger was waiting around every turn at almost every track. A driver knew the worst was possible on every lap. But that was then, and this is now. It's a little like a toddler who has never touched a hot stove—if you've never been burned, you don't believe it can hurt you. Crashing now is something that tears up your car, not your body.

Consequently, that mistaken view has caused a loss of respect among drivers. Slamming into another car is all too common, even on high-speed ovals like Atlanta and Las Vegas. Driver etiquette has changed. A gentlemen's agreement used to limit when and where you rubbed fenders, but courtesy is often a lost gesture. All too often, it's get out of the way or get taken out.

Even at Daytona and Talladega—NASCAR's two most dangerous tracks—some drivers feel invincible, but the older drivers know better. In 2006 at Daytona, Tony Stewart said, "We're going to kill somebody." Hopefully, it doesn't come to that for drivers to understand a tragedy can happen at any moment. Currently, too many of them are willing to take too many chances.

Of course, drivers won't admit this flaw. If you ask them, every single one will say he respects the risks that come with racing cars at 200 mph. The on-track action sometimes doesn't match up with those thoughts. One week after Stewart gave his gruesome warning, he put Matt Kenseth into the wall during the Daytona 500.

The Car of Tomorrow is the safest stock car ever built, protecting drivers in ways that no other car did in the past. The drivers know it, and consequently few drivers expect a tragic outcome. That complacency has become a driver's biggest enemy. The chance of a fatality has been greatly diminished, but it still exists. The more drivers who ignore the danger and race beyond sensible limits, the more likely something tragic will happen.

A little more fear would be a good thing.

CHAPTER 11

The Big Names of NASCAR

A big part of NASCAR's success during the last 20 years has been the ability to market its drivers and make them the star of the show instead of the car. That concept has built enormous loyalty with the fans. If a baseball player signs with another team, the fans of the team he left no longer consider him one of their own. That's not true in NASCAR. Drivers move from team to team, but the fans remain devoted to their guy regardless of the car he pilots or the team he represents.

Driver popularity remains the same regardless of what sponsor is on the hood of their car. These guys are big names any way you look at it. Of course, some of them are bigger than others. But this chapter isn't just about drivers. Some of the biggest names and most influential people in NASCAR have never sat in a race car. Some people you've never heard of do more for the sport than the celebrities who grace the TV screen each week.

Some of those people are listed here, but let's start with the biggest of the big—NASCAR's crown prince.

Most Underrated Active Driver
DALE EARNHARDT JR.

I fooled you on that one, didn't I? So many people think Junior is overrated, and they're all dead wrong. While working on this book, I had more than a few people strongly suggest that I list Earnhardt Jr. as the most overrated driver racing today.

You've all heard the talk: "He's not anywhere near as good as people say." "He's just living off his father's legacy." "He wouldn't even be in Cup if he wasn't named Earnhardt." "He's never going to win a championship." "His name alone makes him popular." "He's never lived up to expectations." I've listened to it for years. And guess what? I don't buy any of it for a second.

Dale Earnhardt Jr. qualified for the NASCAR Sprint Cup Series Coca-Cola 600 auto race at Lowe's Motor Speedway in Concord, North Carolina, on Thursday, May 22, 2008. (AP Photo/Rick Havner)

At the time this book went to print, Earnhardt Jr. ranked second in the Sprint Cup standings, making the most of his first season at Hendrick Motorsports. He was a serious contender for the championship. If he wins it, I'll look like a genius (a hard thing to do). If he doesn't, I don't doubt my selection one iota.

No driver in the history of racing has been under more scrutiny and more pressure than Earnhardt Jr. He is the Elvis of racing. Everything he does, everywhere he goes, every decision he makes, and every lap he races is analyzed, debated, and critiqued.

At the time when his career was just beginning to blossom, he lost the defining figure in his life. Junior finished second in the 2001 Daytona 500 seconds after his father was killed in Turn 4. The man who had guided his every move in racing was gone. Suddenly, Junior had to make his mark on his own.

We all lose our fathers at some point, but we're talking about a living legend of NASCAR, the biggest star in a sport that was undergoing a meteoric rise in popularity. Dale Earnhardt Sr.'s death brought about revolutionary changes in safety and made NASCAR the focus of national attention.

It also put Earnhardt Jr.'s life under a microscope. Overnight, he became NASCAR's top celebrity during the most difficult period of his life. There was no time to grieve. Junior had to try to live up to his father's iconic image.

At the time of his father's death, Earnhardt Jr. had two Cup victories. Over the next four seasons, he would win 13 times. That included the very next race at Daytona, an emotional victory in the 2001 Pepsi 400. The year his father died, Junior finished eighth in the rankings with three victories and 15 top-10 finishes. I'd call that answering the bell when the going got tough.

Junior finished a career-best third in 2003, the year before the Chase playoff was started. He would go on to win the Daytona 500 to start 2004, three years after Dale Sr. was killed. Junior won six times in 2004 and finished fifth in the Cup standings. He had 21 top-10 finishes in 2004, including 16 top-5 finishes. He went to the final race of the season at

Miami with a chance to win the title, sitting fourth in the standings but only 72 points behind leader Kurt Busch.

Earnhardt Jr. was on the cusp of winning a title. He was at the top of his game at age 30, and then everything changed at Dale Earnhardt, Inc. After Junior had numerous feuds with his cousin, car chief Tony Eury Jr., DEI officials made the decision to swap crews and cars with teammate Michael Waltrip. The idea was to make Waltrip a contender and propel Junior to a title.

The decision was a disaster, proving to be the beginning of the end for Junior's time at DEI. He won once in 2005 and finished a career worst 19th in the standings. Junior made the Chase in 2006 but had only one victory all year. He knew things had to change in 2007, the final year of his contract at DEI.

At age 32, Earnhardt Jr. made a decision that changed his life. He wanted to take over controlling interest at DEI from his step-mother, Teresa Earnhardt, or he wanted out. This was a serious confrontation with major financial ramifications. It was an announcement that rocked the sport two weeks before the 2007 season began. Earnhardt's ultimatum surprised most people because few of us had seen that side of him.

Any hint of naiveté was long gone. This was the shrewd Junior, the one playing for keeps. Now he really was his father's son, fighting for what he thought was right. He took an aggressive posture, believing his leadership was the only way DEI was going to become the team his father wanted it to be.

It was a move toward a hostile takeover of a growing company. When Earnhardt Jr. said he wanted majority ownership in DEI, he turned a wheel in the big leagues of the business world, where people do what they must to get what they want. At that moment, the differences with his step-mother moved way beyond a family feud. Earnhardt Jr. was telling Teresa that he should own DEI, that he is DEI, and he could run it better than she had.

Six years after Dale Sr.'s death, Earnhardt Jr. didn't think DEI was where it should be. He had a major problem with Teresa's leadership. He was also upset over her *Wall Street Journal* statement two months earlier, calling it a "low blow." Teresa had said Earnhardt Jr. needed to decide if he wanted to be a race car driver or a public personality.

Apparently, he wanted to be taken seriously as the most important person at DEI. Junior wasn't just a race car driver any longer. He was seen in a different light by rivals, reporters, and fans. Junior separated himself from his past image of the aw-shucks NASCAR star hoping to get a little piece of the family business in his new contract.

That February day we met the new Dale Jr.—the serious, look-you-in-the-eye man who believed it was time to take control of his father's legacy. Earnhardt Jr. was asked on ESPN2 *NASCAR Now* if he wanted 51 percent of DEI. "Actually, 100 percent would be nice," he said, and he wasn't laughing.

Junior said he had a vision of where he wanted DEI to go. But as we found out later, Teresa refused to hand over the keys to the DEI kingdom. She called Junior's bluff. Big mistake. He left, signing the most lucrative deal in NASCAR history, somewhere north of $25 million, to join Hendrick Motorsports.

Budweiser, Earnhardt's Jr.'s sponsor since his rookie season of 2000, also left DEI, but not to join Earnhardt Jr. And that was his choice. Junior, with some guidance from his sister and business manager, Kelley Earnhardt Elledge, realized his brand needed to expand. He couldn't do that with a beer company. It limited what Earnhardt could market to children.

Earnhardt's new sponsors were Amp Energy Drink and the National Guard. He also signed deals with Adidas and Sony. But his decision to leave DEI wasn't about money. It was about winning and racing for someone he respected—Rick Hendrick. Earnhardt knew pressure would come in the switch to Hendrick Motorsports because people would expect him to win a championship.

No excuses. If it doesn't happen, people will have a right to say he wasn't that good. But it was worth the risk for Junior because of what he gained professionally and personally. He went with the man he saw as a father figure. Since Dale Sr.'s death, no one, including Richard Childress, has filled that void better than Rick Hendrick.

"I know my dad would trust Rick," Earnhardt said. "They had great respect for each other. I think he would appreciate what Rick is trying to do for me."

But leaving the company that his father founded wasn't easy for Junior. No doubt he asked himself many times, "What would my dad say?" Anyone who knew Earnhardt Sr. can probably guess. He would tell his son to do what's best for him, not what's best for DEI. It's about being the best driver he can. If that means separating business from family, so be it.

Earnhardt Sr. became an enormous success story because he did what he had to do, even if it caused him problems with family and friends. Childress could tell Junior a thing or two about that. The irony of it all is Junior wouldn't have needed to leave had his father still been around. DEI would have been a stronger and better organization.

Signing with Hendrick Motorsports gave Earnhardt what he felt he didn't have at DEI since his father's death—a boss who cared more about him as a person than a driver. It also gave him the best equipment in the sport and a realistic shot at winning a championship.

Many Earnhardt fans think it was Childress who became Junior's sounding board after his dad died at Daytona. They're wrong, it was Hendrick. The old-school Earnhardt fans wanted him to sign with Childress to try to bring back the past at the place where his father won six of his seven championships. They saw Hendrick, and especially new teammate Jeff Gordon, as the enemy. Junior never felt that way, and neither did his father. Despite what the fans thought, Dale Sr. respected Gordon and admired his talent. They wanted to beat each other, but there was no bad blood between them.

That concept passed down to Dale Jr. Most people didn't know of the close relationship over the years between the Earnhardt family and the Hendrick family. Junior talked about how his grandfather built cars for Rick and helped him get started in racing. But the meaningful relationship between Hendrick and Junior started after Dale Sr. died in 2001. "Rick was always willing to advise me on things," Earnhardt said. "All he cared about was my well-being and me being happy."

When Kelley Earnhardt Elledge, Junior's sister and business manager, was hospitalized earlier this year for surgery to remove a cyst, Hendrick called Junior. "Rick wanted to make sure Kelley was receiving the best possible care," Earnhardt said. "Having been through an illness himself [overcoming leukemia] he really understood how we felt."

Through good times and bad, Hendrick has been there for Earnhardt. Now they have a chance to do something special together by proving that Dale Jr. is one of the best drivers in NASCAR. Despite his carefree image, Earnhardt Jr. wants to win a championship. He wants it badly, but Junior isn't trying to equal his father's seven titles. No one can do that. No one can be Dale Earnhardt Sr. That's the unreachable greatness Junior has to live with as the son of the master.

If his name was John Smith instead of Dale Earnhardt Jr., no one would question his ability. He had 18 Cup victories at midseason of 2008. He finished in the top 10 in the standings four times in six years (2001–06) and was well on his way to doing so again in 2008.

Earnhardt Jr. is much more than just a guy with a famous name who can win a popularity contest. He is one hell of a race car driver.

Most Underrated Person in the NASCAR Hierarchy
BILL FRANCE JR.

Bill France Sr. started NASCAR and made stock car racing a legitimate sport. Bill France Jr. made NASCAR a national sport. In a sentence, that's the legacy of France Jr., who died in 2007 at age 74.

Bill Jr. wasn't just a member of the lucky gene pool. When he took over a successful business from his father in 1972, France Jr. had no desire to sit back and enjoy the ride. More than anyone else, France built NASCAR into the most popular racing series in the country. Few people saw that kind of leadership and drive in France when his father passed him the reins. He was 38, but he didn't have the commanding presence his father possessed.

If you're a junior of a famous father, it's always difficult to live up to expectations. It's even harder if your father was seen as the toughest guy around—ask Dale Earnhardt Jr. Bill Sr. was a bear of a man, 6'5" with a deep voice and a commanding way. He was "Big Bill" to those who knew him. He wasn't the type of man you wanted to cross.

In 1976, A.J. Foyt's qualifying lap for the Daytona 500 was disallowed for using nitrous oxide. Foyt was furious and was screaming at Bill Sr. in the garage. Foyt is an intimidating guy, but he was no match for Big Bill. Four years after his retirement, France Sr. was still a man drivers feared. He drove into the garage area and took Foyt behind closed doors. When they emerged, France had his arm around Foyt's neck and Foyt was saying, "Yes, sir, Mr. France." That was Big Bill. The man could turn a raging bull into a six-week-old poodle.

Bill Jr. was no shrinking violet, but he wasn't Big Bill, not in those days. Bill Jr. had a vision to make NASCAR more than his father ever dreamed it could be. He guided NASCAR through the era when Tobacco Road made NASCAR big business. More than three decades of the Winston Cup through the R.J. Reynolds Tobacco sponsorship raised NASCAR to new heights. The majority of Cup races were not televised when France Jr. took charge, but he was instrumental in getting the TV networks to increase their involvement in the sport.

The 1979 Daytona 500 on CBS was the first flag-to-flag coverage of the event. For France Jr., it was like winning the lottery, thanks to a wild finish and a post-race brawl that piqued the interest of viewers across the country. France Jr. knew it would take more than one crazy brawl between the Allisons and Cale Yarborough to get NASCAR where he wanted it to go.

He temporarily made peace with his biggest rival in an effort to move NASCAR to the next level. Speedway Motorsports Inc. mogul Bruton Smith will never forget the day more than 20 years ago when France Jr. called him to ask an important question. "He asked me if I would help build NASCAR into a national sport," Smith said. "I told him, 'Of course I will.'"

The plan was to build and acquire new speedways in major markets and move races to bigger cities outside the Southeast. It worked. Races moved to major metro areas—Chicago, Kansas City, Southern California, Las Vegas, Miami, and Dallas/Fort Worth.

That last one was the problem. Smith felt France didn't live up to his end of the bargain on Texas Motor Speedway in Fort Worth. Smith said France promised him a Cup date he didn't deliver. France said it never happened, and people saw just how surly he could be. He looked more like Big Bill than ever before.

The disagreement led to a major lawsuit and an eventual second Cup date for Texas. In the end, France and Smith still wanted the same thing— to see NASCAR grow into a major national sport. Before that lawsuit was settled, France Jr.'s health had deteriorated significantly. He passed the reins to his son, Brian, in September of 2003. The France family transition had come full circle. People wondered whether Brian could become the powerful presence his father maintained over the sport.

Eight months after Brian took over, he announced the settlement, giving TMS a second Cup date and eliminating Rockingham, North Carolina, from the schedule. But Bill Jr. was still heavily involved in all major decisions with NASCAR until the end.

When the inaugural 2010 class of the NASCAR Hall of Fame is announced, Bill Jr. is a guaranteed entry. But few people understand that it was Bill Jr., not Bill Sr., who got NASCAR where it is today. France Jr. made NASCAR mainstream. He took the prize Bill Sr. founded and made it bigger, better, and more successful than anyone thought possible. Isn't that what any father would love to say about his son?

Most Underrated Dealmaker
BRUTON SMITH

I've said many times that Bruton Smith is the perfect person to take on a fishing trip. Even if you didn't get a bite the whole weekend, Smith would have a whopper of a tale waiting to regale your buddies upon returning. Like grandpa with a good fishing story, it isn't easy to separate fact from fiction and reality from fantasy when talking to Smith. But the Speedway Motorsports Inc. mogul isn't just hoping to regale you with an entertaining yarn. Everything that comes out of his mouth has an intended purpose for the future.

People sometimes laugh off his talk as Bruton being Bruton, but he usually gets his way. For example, in 2007 when Concord, North Carolina, officials balked at his plans to build a drag racing facility on the grounds at Lowe's Motor Speedway, Smith threatened to shut the place down and move elsewhere.

Did it sound a little crazy? Absolutely. Did the bluff work? You better believe it. The Concord folks were playing way out of their league. Smith got the rights to build his new $60 million drag-racing palace, which debuted with an NHRA event in September.

In the past year alone, Smith has spent $478 million in acquiring and building new venues. He bought New Hampshire Motor Speedway for $340 million and Kentucky Speedway for $78 million. Those purchases were part of the falling out Smith had with long-time Lowe's Motor Speedway president Humpy Wheeler, a legend in the speedway promotion business.

The acquisitions have put a huge debt load on SMI, but Smith is always looking ahead. At age 81 (and no one but Bruton knows if that number is accurate), he still thinks about how things will look 10 years down the road.

Smith is like an old Texas wildcatter who hit the mother lode with his first oil well but uses all that money for the thrill of trying to find another one. He's worth an estimated $1.6 billion, but he isn't happy unless he's plotting his next mega-money move. Smith still has goals for his empire that he hasn't achieved. He wants a second Cup date for Las Vegas and will try to purchase the track at Pocono or Dover to get it, thereby moving one of those Cup dates to Vegas.

He still wants to buy the NHRA, but is waiting until they offer it at a bargain basement price. Give him credit, the man thinks big. Texas Motor Speedway, one of the eight tracks he owns, was his pet project for a long time. Smith finally got the second Cup date he wanted for TMS. It took a bitter lawsuit and a $100 million check to International Speedway Corp. (NASCAR's track management arm) for the track at Rockingham, which Smith shut down to move its Cup date to Texas.

Now Vegas is his top priority, but he knows the second race won't come from NASCAR. The only way to get it is to buy a date from another track. Smith has always maintained that the entertainment capital of the world deserves two races. But he doesn't say NASCAR owes it to him, as he did with TMS. "No one promised me a second date [for Vegas]," Smith said. "But we are asking the wrong questions. The right question is this: 'Is it better for the sport to race twice a year at Vegas?' The answer is absolutely." Smith does everything he can to enhance his stance. He spent $300 million to renovate and reconstruct LVMS, adding banking to the racing surface and making the infield a fan paradise with the Neon Garage. Fans can walk above the Cup garages and look down through a glass roof to see the teams working on the cars.

Smith is the Donald Trump of NASCAR and never fails to say and do the unexpected. He has no concerns about political correctness. He was once asked if he might consider building a racetrack in Mexico. "Not interested," Smith said. "First, I don't speak Spanish. I thought Taco Bell was a telephone company." And that's Bruton—what you see is what you get. Whether it's a one-liner or a carefully crafted lobbying speech, Smith has a story to tell. It's appropriate that he has so much passion for his track in Las Vegas. He's always willing to roll the dice.

Most Underrated Track Executive
GILLIAN ZUCKER

Okay, I know what you're thinking. How can I rate Auto Club Speedway, Zucker's track, as the most overrated facility but list Zucker as underrated? Hey, she didn't build the place in Fontana, the land of warehouses. She also didn't choose the two horrible race dates NASCAR gave her for years—one on the weekend when the Academy Awards are taking place down the road, and the other on Labor Day weekend when temperatures in the Inland Empire make the surface of Mercury look more appealing.

She also didn't build the racing surface, which seeped water onto the pavement during the five-hour rain delay (it wasn't raining at the time) and eventual one-day postponement for the February event in 2008. The truth is Zucker has done everything in her power to make the Fontana facility a quality speedway. She was instrumental in bringing in Auto Club as the title sponsor of the track, bringing in more than $3 million annually.

She has done everything she can to get the Hollywood elite involved and engaged at the track, but the facility lacks the amenities other tracks have to wine and dine the upper crust. Despite all the obstacles NASCAR has thrown at Zucker, she manages to keep a positive attitude and always works toward finding solutions to make the track more popular in Southern California.

Zucker and her staff came up with a great idea to lure the college football fans to the Labor Day weekend Cup race in 2008. It included a combo-ticket package for the race and a ticket to the Tennessee-UCLA football game. Here's what you got for $99:

- A guided tour of the Rose Bowl on Saturday.
- A reserved lower-grandstand seat for the Pepsi 500 on Sunday night. Access to the VIP area at the track and a chance to meet veteran driver Sterling Marlin, a Tennessee native and huge Vols fan.
- A ticket to the Tennessee-UCLA game at the Rose Bowl on Labor Day.

Almost everyone saw the merit in that idea, but Zucker took some heat for a wilder thought after the 2008 February event. She said Michael Waltrip's suggestion of adding banking and making ACS a restrictor-plate track was something worth considering to improve the racing and give the track its own identity.

An ESPN fan poll showed overwhelming support for the idea. Most of the media and virtually everyone at the NASCAR offices in Daytona Beach found it laughable. They all missed the point. Zucker wants to do whatever she can to bring attention to the facility, attract fans, and make it the place it should be for the second largest market in the country. All she needs is a little help from her bosses, who don't seem to appreciate her efforts.

Most Underrated Team Executive
JAY FRYE—TEAM RED BULL GENERAL MANAGER

The first year in Cup for Team Red Bull, the year before Jay Frye arrived, was an embarrassment. The second year after Frye arrived (2008), was the most remarkable turnaround in NASCAR.

Frye spent most of his career trying to guide underfunded teams, always getting the most he could out of situations with limited means. When he arrived at the Red Bull Toyota team, Frye realized things would be different. The budget shocked him, giving him the funding he needed to make the organization successful. But he had a long way to go.

The two-car team had only one top-5 finish in 2007. Rookie driver A.J. Allmendinger qualified for only 17 of 36 races. Brian Vickers, who left Hendrick Motorsports to join Red Bull, failed to qualify for 13 events.

Frye set a plan in motion that has worked amazingly well. Midway through 2008, Vickers was a contender to make the Chase. Allmendinger, after being taken out of the car for five races, returned a new man. He earned his first top 10 at Indianapolis in July.

Everyone in the organization credits Frye with making the struggling operation into a respectable organization. "Jay's been huge for us," Allmendinger said. "He's given the team a lot of structure and a lot of leadership. Last year [2007] there were questions about who was running things and what decisions were being made. Not anymore."

Allmendinger said the keys to Frye's success are honesty and trust. Allmendinger learned early in the 2008 season that he could trust Frye when Frye replaced him in the No. 84 Toyota. Frye put veteran driver Mike Skinner in the car for five races.

"If you get out of the race car, you rarely get back in it," Allmendinger said. "That's sort of the rule of thumb for a race car driver. But Jay was up front with me. He told me that it was still my race car and we just needed to see where we were at. Jay showed me he's a straight-up guy. He was truthful to me. That was a big deal. He's done a lot of great things for this team."

Frye did good things at MB2 Motorsports, which became Ginn Racing when Bobby Ginn bought Frye's operation in 2006. Ginn came with high hopes, adding employees and promising big things. A year later, Ginn was long gone, out of money from a lack of sponsorship. He sold the operation to Dale Earnhardt, Inc. That left Frye in limbo, uncertain about his future.

Toyota Racing's Lee White saw Frye's availability as a golden opportunity for Team Red Bull, recommending Frye to the organization. Before the start of the 2008 season, Frye flew to Austria to meet with Red Bull billionaire owner Dietrich Mateschitz.

Frye went to work using many of the team management skills he learned at Hendrick Motorsports, where his NASCAR career began. Frye brought an organized management system to Red Bull that he saw at Hendrick. He created structure in an organization that was clueless about the ins and outs of NASCAR. But his biggest contribution was an attitude change, adding a team closeness he learned as a college linebacker at Missouri.

Unlike his years at MB2, Frye finally had the funding to put the right people in place. One of them was crew chief Jimmy Elledge, who Frye quickly snapped up to work with Allmendinger when Elledge left Chip Ganassi's team.

Team Red Bull has yet to win, but it's coming. The operation could expand to three cars soon by bringing former Formula One driver Scott Speed to Cup. Frye and Red Bull took things slowly when Speed made the transition from open wheel, learning from the mistakes of other organizations (and Almendinger) of trying to bring open-wheelers directly to Cup.

Frye has paid his dues in NASCAR. Finally, he has a situation where he can display his talent for running a race team.

The Most Underrated Leader in NASCAR
CHAD KNAUS

Jimmie Johnson is a hell of a race car driver, but he wouldn't be a Sprint Cup champion if it wasn't for Chad Knaus. No driver in NASCAR owes more to his crew chief than Johnson. Knaus is more than just the best crew

Crew chief Chad Knaus watches Jimmie Johnson during practice for the NASCAR 3M Performance 400 at Michigan International Speedway in Brooklyn, Michigan, on Friday, August 17, 2007. Knaus and Jeff Gordon's crew chief Steve Letarte were back at the track after six-week suspensions. (AP Photo/Paul Sancya)

chief in NASCAR. He always had the technical skills—so do a lot of guys in the Cup garage—but Knaus made himself a leader who can change the outcome of a race by adjusting to almost any unforeseen situation.

It was Knaus who painted the masterpiece that became back-to-back championships for Johnson in 2006 and 2007. Knaus has reached the pinnacle of his profession, but he admits it took a little soul searching to get there.

When Johnson fell short of a championship for the fourth consecutive year in 2005, the relationship between driver and crew chief had soured. The frustrations over coming so close to the title without winning were almost too much to bear. "The pressure was getting to both of them," said team owner Rick Hendrick. "There wasn't any sense in starting the year [together] if they were not committed to making it work. They had to decide themselves."

Knaus and Johnson decided to give it one more shot in 2006, but Knaus knew he needed to take a different approach to his job as the man making the decisions for the No. 48 Chevy. While covering Banquet Week at New York in 2006 for ESPN.com, Knaus told me how he reevaluated his life. "I put a lot of effort into changing my personal outlook and my team-building outlook," Knaus said. "I knew I was a good crew chief, but I wasn't the best leader I needed to be."

Knaus knew something was missing. It wasn't technical knowledge. It wasn't work ethic or determination. And it wasn't desire. It was too much of everything. "Chad was working himself to death," Johnson said. "He was burning himself out. We all knew things had to change."

Knaus began delegating more responsibilities to other members of the team, but he was forced to do more delegating than he planned at the start of the 2006 season. His amazing technical skills went a step too far in Daytona. A post-qualifying inspection revealed an innovative, but illegal, alteration. Knaus had figured out a way to change the height of the car without using an extra part.

NASCAR inspectors weren't impressed. Knaus was sent home for four weeks and fined $25,000. He watched on TV as his team won the Daytona 500. "It hurt, but it also was the proudest moment of my life," Knaus said. "I was like a parent sending his kid off to kindergarten for the first time. Guys that I raised here since they were 18 years old won the Daytona 500 without me.

"But I learned one other thing that day. Not being there made me realize I wanted to do what I do more than anything in the world."

Knaus returned with a new zeal for his job, and sometimes that zeal puts him over the edge in NASCAR's eyes. Critics say he's a cheater, but Knaus is what every crew chief wants to be—a brilliant innovator who finds ways to make his car faster by pushing the rules to the limit.

Knaus faced another suspension in 2007 when the fenders on the car didn't fit the template. Jeff Gordon's car had the same problem, no surprise since those cars are built in the same shop by the same guys. By that time, Knaus had learned his team could get things done without him being at the track. The team kept running well because Knaus set them free. He realized he couldn't do everything himself.

"I was micro-managing," Knaus said. "By the time we got to the end of the season [in 2005], I was whipped. I had to allow my guys to do things without me going back and double-checking everybody. I had to trust them and make them responsible for their areas."

The trust helped Knaus build the most efficient team in NASCAR. But he also had to trust someone else a little more—Johnson. "I'm real proud of them because we went through some pretty tough times," Hendrick said. "Honestly, I think they are as good a driver-crew chief combination as I've ever had in racing."

Hendrick has witnessed the best of the best with Ray Evernham and Gordon. They won three championships together, and Knaus was part of that success. He was fabricator and a tire changer for the No. 24 team, learning to do things the Evernham way before Evernham moved on to become a team owner.

When Johnson clinched the title at Homestead-Miami Speedway, Evernham was the first person to hug Knaus in Victory Lane. "Ray is probably the most driven person I've ever met in my life," Knaus said. "I respect him so much. I modeled my crew-chief style after him. But I found that just wasn't working for me. I knew I had to change."

Knaus' days as a workaholic came to an end. He sees things differently now, concentrating on the big picture. He finally realized there was more to life than being a crew chief. Ironically, that made him a better crew chief and a better man. He learned to enjoy life. After Johnson won his second Cup title in 2007, Knaus treated himself to an expensive new toy. Hendrick was the first person to hear about it, receiving a call from Knaus during a luncheon in New York. "I remember what crew chiefs made back in the day," Hendrick said. "But that call was from Chad. He said he stopped and bought a Maserati, so I guess things are at a new level."

Top Five NASCAR Leaders
1. TEAM OWNER RICHARD CHILDRESS

Had to overcome the death of the sport's biggest star in Dale Earnhardt Sr. and rebuild his organization. Earnhardt was more than just a driver to Childress. The two men were like brothers, building one of the top teams in NASCAR at Richard Childress Racing. They won six Cup championships together.

Richard Childress looks out from the garage during practice for the NASCAR Nextel Cup Series Coca-Cola 600 auto race at Lowe's Motor Speedway in Concord, North Carolina, on Thursday, May 24, 2007. (AP Photo/Terry Renna)

Childress didn't know if he wanted to continue to race after Earnhardt died. But he felt he owed it to all his employees, and he knew working to stay competitive is what Earnhardt would have wanted. Childress hired driver Jeff Burton, a man whom Earnhardt had singled out as someone RCR should target. Burton helped turn the operation around. All three RCR drivers—Burton, Kevin Harvick, and Clint Bowyer—made the Chase in 2007.

Childress is adding a fourth car in 2009 and has full sponsorship for all four cars, not an easy thing to do in a soft economy, but it says a lot for the respect Childress has earned in his career.

2. TEXAS MOTOR SPEEDWAY PRESIDENT EDDIE GOSSAGE

Almost everyone in NASCAR has a story to tell about Gossage—and that's how Gossage wants it. He often makes himself the center of attention, which some people see as self-aggrandizing. That's not Gossage's goal. His genius is keeping TMS front and center at every possible moment, not an easy thing to do when he only has three major race weekends a year—two for NASCAR and one for the IndyCar Series.

Gossage isn't afraid to say what he really thinks, even if it means criticizing NASCAR policies or major NASCAR decisions. That's why people listen to him. He doesn't just spout the party line. Whether you agree with Gossage or not, he always makes any major issue interesting.

NASCAR needs more track promoters like Gossage who keep the sport in the public eye and never stop thinking of ways to make NASCAR better.

3. TEAM OWNER RICK HENDRICK

One of the most well-liked and respected men in the sport, Hendrick has managed to build a NASCAR super team with drivers Jeff Gordon, Jimmie Johnson, Dale Earnhardt Jr., and Mark Martin. It won't be easy to keep all four superstars happy, but if anyone can do it, Hendrick can. Hendrick runs his team the way a good father handles his children. He has a calm demeanor and shows all his 500 employees that he cares about their well-being. But Hendrick also insists on total discipline in a structured environment where everyone contributes.

4. TEAM OWNER JOE GIBBS

Who else could put up with Tony Stewart's temper tantrums for 11 years? Who else could take wild-man racer Kyle Busch and make him a championship contender and a consistent winner?

Gibbs transferred his skills as a championship football coach into building one of the most successful organizations in NASCAR. That success continued when Gibbs returned to coaching after the Washington Redskins made him an offer he couldn't refuse. Gibbs already had the man in place to run the show—his son, J.D. Gibbs.

Joe Gibbs is back now, and the team continues to make the right decisions for the future. The organization was criticized for leaving Chevrolet to become a Toyota team, with people wondering whether or not the team could continue to contend. It was a brilliant move that made Joe Gibbs Racing Toyota's top team instead of Chevy's third or fourth team. Gibbs knew that people win races, not manufacturers, and he had the right people in place to win immediately with Toyota.

Gibbs also made the right decision to let Stewart out of his contract and become a team owner in 2009. Never keep a guy who doesn't want to be there. Besides, Gibbs had a superstar-in-the-making waiting to take over the No. 20 Camry in Joey Logano, the most celebrated teenage driver in NASCAR history.

5. JEFF GORDON

No driver in the history of the sport has done more to bring NASCAR into the mainstream of national popularity than Gordon. He almost single-handedly changed the image of NASCAR and made many casual fans realize that NASCAR offered more than the Southern hillbilly stereotype. Gordon's polished and poised demeanor made him a celebrity outside of racing, and he has hosted TV shows and become a spokesman for products that never would have considered NASCAR sponsorship without him.

His rivalry with Dale Earnhardt Sr. propelled the sport to new heights. Earnhardt was the working-class hero, and Gordon was the hated outsider that the old-school fans jeered. To his credit, it was Gordon who stepped up and became one of the leaders in the garage after Earnhardt died. He offered his opinions on the key issues of the moment, unafraid to criticize NASCAR when he felt it was deserved.

Whenever he speaks and whatever he says, Gordon always conducts himself with class. He was exactly what NASCAR needed to grow beyond its Southern roots. Gordon still receives his share of boos from the fans when he's introduced before the race, but most of the people who boo him understand that he has made NASCAR a bigger and better sport.

CHAPTER 12

Cars and Trophies

This is the fun chapter—or maybe I should say the make-fun-of chapter. If there's one aspect of NASCAR that almost every race fan has an opinion on, it's paint schemes for the cars of their favorite drivers. Some people like to keep it simple, and some like it wild and crazy.

For some cars, these colors change more often than the late afternoon weather in July at Daytona. Most of the big teams have multiple paint schemes these days to highlight sponsors' needs in specific markets. Teams often use one-off schemes for races under the lights, promoting everything from movie premieres to the MLB All-Star Game.

Some paint schemes are quite elaborate, sometimes too elaborate. That's the biggest problem in NASCAR paint schemes today—they're just too busy. The cars have so much information packed onto the sheet metal that it's like trying to read hieroglyphics. But sponsors and team owners go all out because they realize brand loyalty is huge for NASCAR fans. They buy what they see circling the track over and over again.

It works best when you don't make it too difficult for fans to figure out. Some cars have so many colors mixed together that you would think the car just slammed into the wall of a paint factory. Other cars are just plan boring, usually because the sponsor colors leave something to be desired, but if the message is obvious, they don't really care. Everyone knew what the sponsor did on the Yellow Transportation car in the former

Busch Series, even though the car and the sponsor color wasn't yellow. It was a dull orange.

Variety is what NASCAR paint schemes are all about. The more paint scheme variations you have, the more die-cast cars you can sell on the shopping channels. They even sell die-cast cars with paint schemes that never actually made it into a race.

There's something for everyone. The same is true of NASCAR trophies for winning races. Trophies have become a keeping-up-with-the-Joneses thing as many speedways attempt to offer the biggest, most unusual, or most expensive thing to give the winner in Victory Lane. Some trophies are major pieces of prized artwork. Some are things you wouldn't see at a flea market. And some have sentimental value for the winner and the speedway.

Some tracks have established a great tradition that has endured through the years. Others simply go with whatever the title sponsor of the race wants to use to help promote the brand. At one track, the car and trophy go together. We'll explain, but here are some paint schemes and trophies that stand out.

Most Overrated Paint Scheme
THE NO. 17 DEWALT FORD OF MATT KENSETH

It's bad enough that NASCAR takes criticism from a few snooty Formula One fans who consider the sport glorified taxi cab racing, so don't add fuel to the flame by racing a car that actually looks like a taxi cab.

I realize the dull yellow and black combo are the corporate colors for DeWalt, but spice up the car a little somehow. Even Kenseth's personality, nice but not exactly the life of the party, has more pizzazz than the look on the No. 17 machine.

This car certainly accomplishes the goal of sponsor recognition. You equate yellow and black power tools to that Ford Kenseth drives every week. Clearly, pink and fuchsia won't work when you're selling manly tools, but jazzing it up a little wouldn't hurt.

Matt Kenseth during Daytona 500 qualification at the Daytona International Speedway in Daytona Beach, Florida, on Sunday, February 10, 2008. Dewalt's plain yellow-and-black paint scheme isn't a favorite. (AP Photo/Paul Kizzle)

The Rest of the Top Five
2. THE NO. 11 FEDEX TOYOTA OF DENNY HAMLIN

Have you ever seen a black FedEx truck or plane? I didn't think so. For some strange reason, all of Hamlin's cars are black. Joe Gibbs Racing does dress it up a little with some varying colors on the side and the FedEx logo—at least DeWalt sticks to its business colors, even if they are boring. Why doesn't FedEx go with a white scheme with its various purple, orange, green, whatever accompanying colors we see on its equipment and envelopes?

Black is fine and works well on many cars, but not if the sponsor's main color is white. What is Hamlin's ride, a photo negative of FedEx?

3. THE NO. 43 CHEERIOS DODGE DRIVEN BY BOBBY LABONTE

Sky blue, yellow, and red do not go together. This hideous theme will change for Petty Enterprises in 2009 because General Mills is moving to the No. 33 Chevy, the new fourth car for Richard Childress Racing.

Petty Enterprises wanted to leave Richard's traditional baby blue color as part of the new paint scheme, but it just doesn't work with the colors of the Cheerios banner. It looks like someone forgot to repaint part of the car. And it doesn't make me want to go out and eat a bowl of cereal. Here's a little advice to the RCR folks and General Mills: Trash this paint combination for the new ride.

4. THE NO. 15 MENARDS CHEVROLET DRIVEN BY PAUL MENARD

Somebody give me some sunglasses. The bright yellow or fluorescent yellow-green or surface of the sun color, or whatever it is, causes pain in the pupils of your eyes if you look at it too long.

You have to feel for Paul Menard a little on this one. His dad is the sponsor. Tough to say no in that situation to whatever paint scheme the old man wants for your ride. The good news is you won't have any trouble finding Menard on the track. If the lights fail during a night event, just move the No. 15 Chevy to the front to lead the way.

5. NO. 31 CATERPILLAR CHEVY DRIVEN BY JEFF BURTON

Richard Childress Racing had a golden opportunity to correct this ugly scheme when the sponsorship moved from Bill Davis Racing and Dave Blaney's car to Burton's ride.

The big debut with the new car came in July 2008 and, drum roll please, it looked almost the same as before. Whoopee. What a downer. The car looks like the cousin of Matt Kenseth's No. 17 Dewalt Ford—another taxi cab, except with a little red added in. Yeah, that helped.

This theme has now become a family tradition since big brother Ward Burton drove it for several years. Ward won the Daytona 500 with this paint scheme, so maybe that will work for Jeff.

Most Underrated Paint Scheme
THE NO. 24 DUPONT CHEVROLET OF JEFF GORDON

The rainbow theme of Gordon's ride has been criticized by thousands of fans as a little too "sissy-fied" for the macho world of NASCAR. The theme was so outside the norm that it stuck. Gordon's championship pit crew became known as the Rainbow Warriors, a rare example of a crew being named after the paint scheme.

Jeff Gordon crosses the finish line at Michigan Speedway in Brooklyn, Michigan, on Sunday, August 16, 1998, to win the Pepsi 400 NASCAR race. The car's distinctive paint scheme is hard to miss. (AP Photo/Roger Hart)

Few drivers in history have managed to stay with one basic theme for their entire career, but that appears likely now for Gordon. The design has varied some over the years, going from the rainbow colors across the hood to the flames on the car when Gordon won the 2001 championship, but the basic red, blue, and yellow theme has remained the same. The oval Dupont logo has become as big a part of Gordon's brand as STP was for Richard Petty.

Gordon runs other sponsor cars at times with the blue Pepsi car or the bright green Nicorette Chevrolet. The shock of seeing that color alone should help you quit smoking. But it's the DuPont Chevy that people will remember as Gordon's ride long after his racing days are over.

The Rest of the Top Five

2. THE NO. 8 BUDWEISER CHEVROLET OF DALE EARNHARDT JR.

Sorry, but the new Bud car with Kasey Kahne as the driver just isn't the same. The design differences are subtle, but the match-up between sponsor and driver just doesn't work as it did with Junior. Kahne looks more like a boy scout than a beer drinker. I don't think the guys at the frat house are choosing a cold Bud because Kahne promotes the beverage.

Earnhardt Jr., however, is a beer-guzzling kind of guy. I mean, the man owns a bar, for goodness sake. No doubt Earnhardt still throws down a few cold ones with his buds (no pun intended), but he realized he needed to broaden his brand when he made the switch to Hendrick Motorsports.

All that aside, the paint scheme in the Dale Earnhardt, Inc. version of the Bud car was better. The numbers of Junior's ride had a 3-D effect, and DEI's symbol of the elongated "E" ran through the "8" on each door panel, giving the appearance of speed stretching out the letters.

3. THE NO. 51 BOUDREAUX BUTT PASTE DODGE DRIVEN BY KIM CROSBY

Do you really have to ask why this car made the list? That sponsor name will live in NASCAR lore forever. The red-and-yellow paint scheme was nothing special, but the name is a classic.

In case you're wondering, and I'm sure you are, the sponsor product is a diaper rash cream, which is also used for acne, bed sores, shingles, poison ivy, and even lip balm. Not sure I'd want to put something on my lips that has "Butt Paste" in the title, but to each his or her own.

The medication was developed by a Louisiana pharmacist, Dr. George Boudreaux, and the driver of the car was one of the few women to compete in NASCAR. Crosby was a former school principal in Louisiana. The car wasn't around long, but it was fun while it lasted.

4. THE NO. 24 CHAMELEON-THEME CAR FOR JEFF GORDON IN 1998

This was a special paint scheme and one of the most unusual ideas ever for a car color. It was officially known as the Chromalusion car, which Gordon used in the 1998 Winston All-Star race.

The car looked gold in the daylight, but it changed into a reddish purple under the lights at night, depending on which angle you saw it. Gordon ran the chameleon paint in a few other color schemes over the years that changed from violet to blue to green.

It looked cool, like a metallic lizard on the run. Only one problem: Really expensive if he wrecked it and not practical as a selling point with the fans. Be prepared to add a second mortgage on your home if you want to use this paint on your own car—it's $30 for an ounce of the stuff.

5. THE NO. 40 COORS LIGHT DODGE FOR CHIP GANASSI RACING

No matter who was driving it, the Silver Bullet never won much, but it did look like a flying beer can. The car didn't have a great mix of colors, just the Coors silver with the red letters and numbers, along with the Colorado Rockies on the quarter panels at the back. It was sleek and simple, a perfect representation of the sponsor's product that looked stylish all around.

Coors Light left Ganassi's team to become the official beer of NASCAR. In case you didn't know it, NASCAR has an "official" designation for almost everything. Going official meant that the Silver Bullet car would no longer streak down the track.

Top Five Paint Schemes in History

1. THE NO. 3 GM GOODWRENCH CHEVROLET OF DALE EARNHARDT

Is there any doubt? No theme ever fit a driver better than the classic black Earnhardt drove for his last four Cup championships. The Intimidator belonged in black as much as Johnny Cash. The car became unmistakable and synonymous with Earnhardt's rough-and-tough image.

2. THE NO. 43 STP PLYMOUTH/DODGE OF RICHARD PETTY

The baby-blue ride that Petty made famous with the STP oval on the hood. The cars also incorporated some red into the theme over the years, but this ride was a symbol of the Petty family's racing excellence for many years.

The Goodwrench Service Chevrolet pit crew work feverishly during a pit stop with Dale Earnhardt behind the wheel who went on to win the second Twin 125 qualifying race for the Daytona 500 on Thursday, February 16, 1995, in Daytona Beach, Florida.
(AP Photo/Phil Coale)

3. THE NO. 28 TEXACO/HAVOLINE THUNDERBIRD OF DAVEY ALLISON'S 1987 ROOKIE SEASON

A rare instance where multiple contrasting colors worked to perfection. The car was white in front and black in the back, with a little red in between. It had the famous Texaco star on the hood in red, but the things that really stood out were the mirror-like numbers on the sides.

4. THE NO. 92 FABULOUS HUDSON HORNET OF HERB THOMAS

This was one cool car more than 50 years ago. The full name was written in white across the door panels of the unusual blue/gray coloring on the car. "Hornet" was listed in giant letters when Thomas won the 1951 championship. The No. 92 was written on both ends of the lettering.

5. THE NO. 11 MOUNTAIN DEW BUICK OF DARRELL WALTRIP

The car had a unique paint design with its green and white mix. The hood, roof, and rear deck lid were green in the middle, but the edges were white. The door panels were green with white numbers, but the rear quarter panels were white with green and red letters. Dale Earnhardt Jr. has a similar theme now with his Amp Energy car. The drink is a division of Mountain Dew.

Most Underrated Trophy
THE MONSTER AT DOVER INTERNATIONAL SPEEDWAY

There's nothing better for a track known as the Monster Mile than a trophy featuring a big, angry creature awaiting the guy in Victory Lane. The winner gets a trophy that looks a lot like the Incredible Hulk, but he's gray instead of green. Actually, it looks a little like NASCAR president Mike Helton when he's mad at the media, which is most of the time.

The monster is 30" high and weighs 40 pounds—sort of a Mini-Me on steroids, but that's not the best part. A die-cast model of the winner's car is placed in the right hand of the monster. The base of the trophy has the winner's name, the track's emblem, and the name of the race.

Here is Kyle Busch's monster trophy for winning the NASCAR Sprint Cup Best Buy 400 auto race, on Sunday, June 1, 2008, at Dover International Speedway in Dover, Delaware. (AP Photo/Russ Hamilton)

The trophy is so popular that Dover officials also added a monster statue in the infield in 2008 known as "Miles the Monster." The gigantic five-story fiberglass structure, with glowing red eyes, was built by ACI Composites. The statue has a full-size car in his hand.

The Rest of the Top Five
2. THE GRANDFATHER CLOCK AT MARTINSVILLE SPEEDWAY

This is one of the only trophies that the winner can't pick up and hold over his head. Martinsville officials came up with the idea in 1964 when

NASCAR Nextel Cup DirecTV auto race winner Tony Stewart poses with the trophy, a grandfather clock, at the Martinsville Speedway in Martinsville, Virginia, on Sunday, April 2, 2006 (AP Photo/John Harrelson)

an area shop—Ridgeway Clock Company—made one of its masterpieces for Fred Lorenzen when he won on the paper-clip oval in September of that year.

The actual clock the winner receives is shipped to his home a few weeks after his victory. The retail price of these magnificent clocks is around $11,000. It chimes "God Bless America" and "America the Beautiful." So I guess Richard Petty, who won 12 times at Martinsville after 1964, doesn't have any problems knowing what time it is at his house—but all that ticking and chiming might get annoying.

3. COWBOY HATS, BOOTS, AND GUNS AT TEXAS MOTOR SPEEDWAY

Yee-haw boys. When you win on the Fort Worth oval, you know you're in Texas because you're going to act the way that people think Texans do—wear big hats, big boots, and shoot big guns. Every winner receives a cowboy hat to wear in Victory Lane. And every winner since 2005 gets a pair of Beretta pistols, which he symbolically shoots in the air like a drunken cattle rancher. The gun gifts also include a Beretta rifle for any Cup driver who wins a pole at TMS.

The winner of the spring Cup race gets a trophy of hand-carved and hand-painted cowboy boots, including spurs. The winner of the fall event receives a sterling silver cowboy hat as the trophy.

4. THE CHAMPIONSHIP BELT AT LAS VEGAS MOTOR SPEEDWAY

A winner of a Cup race at Las Vegas is the heavyweight champion of NASCAR, even if it's a tiny guy like Jeff Gordon. Winners get a championship belt, similar to what a boxer gets for earning a world title.

The belt has real diamonds and rubies and costs around $3,000. Drivers love this one because they can prance around saying they out-fought the other guys to get it. The winner's name is etched into the belt as soon as he crosses the finish line.

Track officials originally considered a slot-machine trophy but wisely went with the boxing belt. Probably not a good idea to give a trophy that symbolizes an athlete placing a wager.

NASCAR driver Carl Edwards celebrates Texas-style after winning the NASCAR Sprint Cup Series' Dickies 500 auto race at Texas Motor Speedway on Sunday, November 2, 2008, in Fort Worth, Texas. (AP Photo/Tony Gutierrez)

5. THE GUITAR AT NASHVILLE SUPERSPEEDWAY

This instrument goes to the Nationwide Series winner since Nashville doesn't have a Cup race—and this is no dime-store toy for some silly picking in the backyard. The guitar is a Gibson Les Paul beauty. Sam Bass, the officially licensed artist of NASCAR, designs the specific artwork on the guitar for each event.

This is a Carl Edwards favorite. He's quite an accomplished guitar player, so the trophy gave him a little extra incentive to win at Nashville races three consecutive times starting in 2006.

HONORABLE MENTION: THE GIANT BEAR TROPHY AT ATLANTA MOTOR SPEEDWAY

I normally don't think trophies should be sponsor-related, but Bass Pro Shops came up with a doozie one year with the giant bear trophy. The life-size grizzly bear was mounted on a 4-foot high block of wood.

It was part of a wildlife theme Bass Pro Shops had while sponsoring the Atlanta event. One year was a large-mouth bass trophy. Okay, maybe that was stretching it a bit, but the big bear certainly got your attention.

Most Overrated Trophy
THE HARLEY J. EARL TROPHY FOR THE DAYTONA 500

The trophy is named after the renowned General Motors designer who was a good friend of NASCAR founder Bill France Sr. No problem there, Earl deserves recognition. But the top of the trophy features the futuristic car, the Fireball One, which Harley Earl designed in 1954.

It's a cool ride, but it doesn't really have anything to do with racing stock cars at Daytona. It's more like Speed Racer's car or something guys use to set records on the Bonneville Salt Flats. The vehicle on the trophy is silver, but the 50th anniversary trophy was gold. The winner's name goes on the permanent trophy, which stays at Daytona. So does the winner's car.

The good news is all the key players get a trophy. The winner receives a replica of the Earl Trophy. The winning crew chief gets the Cannonball

Ryan Newman raises the trophy in victory lane after winning the Daytona 500 NASCAR Sprint Cup Series auto race at Daytona International Speedway in Daytona Beach, Florida, Sunday, February 17, 2008. (AP Photo/Terry Renna)

Baker Trophy (he was the first commissioner of NASCAR), and the winning owner receives the Governor's Cup.

The Rest of the Top Five
2. THE GOLD BRICK AT INDIANAPOLIS MOTOR SPEEDWAY

Just calling it that makes it overrated. The top of the trophy is just a gold rectangular block. It's supposed to be a brick for The Brickyard, which is a good idea, but a real brick would look better.

The speedway folks could dig up some of those original bricks from the track, maybe set a car on top of it, and give that to each winner, but a gold brick is more appropriate for someone retiring from Fort Knox.

3. ARIZONA DEPICTION TROPHY AT PHOENIX INTERNATIONAL RACEWAY

This thing is as lame as they come. The trophy is basically a plaque in the shape of the state of Arizona (which is pretty much a square) sitting on a wood base. I think the winner at my local go-kart track last weekend got a nicer prize.

A better idea would be a gold Phoenix, the bird that symbolizes fire and divinity. It rises from the ashes, like cars do at times after a crash in Turn 2 on the PIR 1-mile oval.

The Phoenix is a mythical bird with a tail of blue and gold plumage. It has a 1,000-year life cycle, similar to Kyle Petty's Cup career. Near the end of the bird's existence (as the story goes) the Phoenix builds a nest of cinnamon twigs and ignites it. The nest and the bird burn to ashes, and a young Phoenix arises. Now that's a trophy, especially if you could figure out how to set the thing on fire and have it remain in pristine condition when the flames burned out.

4. THE *BATMAN BEGINS* 400 TROPHY AT MICHIGAN INTERNATIONAL SPEEDWAY

In general, naming trophies after sponsors is a bad idea. Here one year, gone the next. Having some guy show up in a Batman costume before the race was entertaining, but the trophy wasn't up to Hollywood standards. It was so weird it's hard to describe. It had some copper thing that looked like horns with black bat wings across the front.

A better idea would have been a scale-size Batmobile (maybe the size of those Shriner's cars in parades) with the winner's name written on the door. Or even better, a Batmobile golf cart. Jimmie Johnson would love that. He could wear a Batman cape and jump off the roof, hopefully not breaking his wrist as he did on an earlier golf cart incident.

5. THE SOARING TROPHY AT KANSAS SPEEDWAY

What the heck is that thing? It's called, *"Soaring"* and was designed by Canadian sculptor May Marx. I think it's some kind of bronze wings, but it looks a little like a burned-up piston on a Cup car when the crew chief says, "We blowed up."

Jeff Gordon holds up the trophy for the NASCAR Protection One 400 at Kansas Speedway in Kansas City, Kansas, on Sunday, September 29, 2002. What the heck is that thing? (AP Photo/Charlie Riedel)

Soaring is a nice piece for a modern art museum in Seattle, but it doesn't fit for a Sprint Cup race winner in Kansas City, Kansas. Here's a thought: How about a twirling house on top of a bronze tornado? Call it the Wizard of Oz Trophy and have it handed out in Victory Lane by the Lion, the Scarecrow, the Tin Man, and Dorothy. The trophy could read, "It takes Courage, Heart, and Brains to go home again and win at Kansas."

References

The following references were consulted for statistical analysis in *The Blount Report*:

ESPN.com
NASCAR Sprint Cup media guide
NASCARmedia.com
Racing-Reference.info
NASCAR.com
Jayski.com.